THE HERMENEUTICS OF PHILO AND HEBREWS

BASEL STUDIES OF THEOLOGY
edited by the Faculty of Theology, Basel
No. 1

THE HERMENEUTICS
OF PHILO AND HEBREWS

*A Comparison of the Interpretation
of the Old Testament in Philo Judaeus
and the Epistle to the Hebrews*

BY

SIDNEY G. SOWERS

JOHN KNOX PRESS · RICHMOND, VIRGINIA

Library of Congress Catalog Card Number: 65-10146
Joint publication by
EVZ-Verlag, Zürich, and John Knox Press, Richmond, Virginia
© EVZ-Verlag, Zürich, 1965

Printing-office Schüler Ltd., Bienne, Switzerland

Preface

This dissertation was written while I was a student in the University of Basel during the years 1960–1962. I wish to thank the Committee on Graduate Fellowships of the United Presbyterian Church in the U.S.A. for having made possible this stay and my subsequent study in the University of Zurich. Except for the encouragement and help of the president of my theological seminary, Dr. Theodore Gill, I probably would not have seen this doctoral program through. I am also indebted to the patient and kind help of my major professor, Dr. Oscar Cullmann, and to Prof. Bo Reicke for several fine suggestions. My thanks go to the Theological Faculty of the University of Basel for accepting this work into its series published by the EVZ-Verlag of Zurich. I am grateful to the University of Basel, the Committee on Graduate Fellowships, and the Mt. Baker Presbyterian Church of Concrete, Washington for their generous help in financing this dissertation's publication.

Except for the passages I have translated myself, the Bible text in this publication is from the *Revised Standard Version of the Bible*, copyrighted 1946 and 1952 by the Division of Christian Education, National Council of Churches, and was used by permission.

Sidney Sowers

Table of Contents

Abbreviations 9

Chapter I: The Impulse to Allegorize 11

  1: Origins of Greek Allegorical Method 11
  2: Alexandrian Jewish Allegory Before Philo 14
  3: Philo's Place in the Allegorical Tradition 19
  4: Philo's Vindication of Allegory. 22

Chapter II: Uncovering the Hidden Meaning 28

  1: The Two-Level View of Scripture. 28
  2: The Inspiration of the Prophets 34
  3: Prophecy as a Mystical Interpretation of Scripture 40

Chapter III: Interpretation of the Law 44

  1: The Law Beyond the Torah 44
  2: The Spiritualization of the Law 49

Chapter IV: The Symbolism of the Sanctuary 55

  1: The Temple Apology 55
  2: The Allegory of the High Priest and His Clothing 58
  3: The Inward Temple and High Priest 62

Chapter V: The Alexandrian Jewish Background to the Epistle to the Hebrews 64

  1: The Background Problem 64
  2: Common Text 66
  3: Reflections of the Philonic Doctrine of the Logos. 66
  4: The Activities of the High Priest 69
  5: The Divine Oath 70

6: Other Convergences of Philo and Hebrews   71
7: The Anti-Judaic Debate   73

Chapter VI: The Christological Fulfillment of Scripture . .   75

1: Prophetic Inspiration and Interpretation   75
2: Old Testament Witnesses to Christ   79

Chapter VII: The Typological Parallel of Two Covenants .   89

1: The Concept of Typological Exegesis   89
2: The Understanding of the Law   97
3: The Shadow of the Heavenly and Eschatological Cult   105
4: Perfection of the Covenant   112
5: Old Testament Types of Christ   115

Chapter VIII: The Parenetic Typology   127

1: The Parenesis of the Lesser to the Greater   127
2: Parenetic Examples   129
3: Chapter Eleven   132

Conclusion   137

Appendix   139

Bibliography   141

Indices   147

Abbreviations

To Philo's works:

Abr.	*On Abraham.*
Aet.	*On the Eternity of the World.*
Agr.	*On Husbandry.*
Apo.	*Hypothetica*
Cher.	*On the Cherubim.*
Conf.	*On the Confusion of Tongues.*
Cont.	*On the Contemplative Life.*
Cong.	*On Mating with the Preliminary Studies.*
Dec.	*On the Decalogue.*
Det.	*That the Worse is Wont to Attack the Better.*
Ebr.	*On Drunkenness.*
Flac.	*Against Flaccus.*
Fug.	*On Flight and Finding.*
Gig.	*On the Giants.*
Her.	*Who is the Heir of Divine Things?*
Immut.	*On the Unchangeableness of God.*
Jos.	*On Joseph.*
LA	*Allegorical Interpretation of Genesis II, III.*
Legat.	*Legation to Gaius.*
Mig.	*On the Migration of Abraham.*
Mos.	*On the Life of Moses.*
Mut.	*On the Change of Names.*
Opif.	*On the Account of the World's Creation Given by Moses.*
Plant.	*On Noah's Work as a Planter.*
Post.	*On the Posterity of Cain and his Exile.*
Praem.	*On Rewards and Punishments.*
Prob.	*That Every Virtuous Man is Free.*
Prov.	*On Providence*
QE	*Questions and Answers on Exodus.*
QG	*Questions and Answers on Genesis.*

Sac.	On the Sacrifices of Abel and Cain.
Sobr.	On Sobriety.
Som.	On Dreams.
Spec.	On the Special Laws.

To literature:

BZAW	Beihefte zur Zeitschrift für die alttestamentliche Wissenschaft.
BZNW	Beihefte zur Zeitschrift für die neutestamentliche Wissenschaft.
CQ	Classical Quarterly.
CR	Classical Review.
ET	The Expository Times.
HUCA	Hebrew Union College Annual.
JBL	Journal of Biblical Literature and Exegesis.
JE	Jewish Encyclopedia.
NTS	New Testament Studies.
RB	Revue Biblique.
RE	Real-Enzyklopädie der klassischen Altertumswissenschaft.
RGG	Die Religion in Geschichte und Gegenwart.
TB	Theologische Blätter.
TL	Theologische Literaturzeitung.
TSK	Theologische Studien und Kritiken.
TWNT	Theologisches Wörterbuch zum Neuen Testament.
ZNW	Zeitschrift für die neutestamentliche Wissenschaft und die Kunde der älteren Kirche.

CHAPTER I

The Impulse to Allegorize

The subject of hermeneutics is one very much discussed today in New Testament studies. Partly owing to Martin Heidegger's special use of the term, the word today often implies not just interpretation of texts, but a whole understanding and interpretation of life, the world, and oneself as well. In this paper we will try to avoid present-day refinements of this kind, and will remain with what classically was at least a primary sense of the word. Hermeneutics as used here means simply, the interpretation and method of interpreting scripture.

Two remarkable and historically important subjects in the history of exegesis are Philo of Alexandria and the author of the Epistle to the Hebrews. To compare their methods of Biblical interpretation and certain points in their exegeses, which will be our task, we must see the positions they occupy in a hermeneutical tradition reaching far back into religious and philosophical antiquity. This is the tradition of allegorical interpretation.

1: Origins of Greek Allegorical Method

The first century Stoic allegorist, Heraclitus, defined allegory as "a style speaking certain things and meaning something other than what it says."[1] Although the word can refer to a style of writing using symbols with hidden meanings and intentions, the historic importance of allegory among the ancients, Jews, Christians, Moslems, and Indians, has been its use as a means of interpreting ancient scriptures and documents. It works from the notion that the writers in former times composed their works in veiled language, writing one thing, intending something else, so

---

[1] *Homeric Questions*, 5.

that their stories, laws, poems, and prophecies become continuous metaphors requiring symbolic interpretation to decipher their true and hidden meanings.[2] This is allegorical interpretation.

The word ἀλληγορία is rather late in the Greek language, and seems to be first used by the Stoic Cleanthes in the third century B.C.[3] It is the later equivalent for an earlier term used by Heracliteans, Sophists, Stoics, and Cynics, ὑπονοία.[4]

The actual origin of allegorical interpretation is somewhat obscure. On the basis of Neo-Pythagorean practices of interpreting a moral doctrine out of a painting located in a temple, E. Bréhier suggests that allegorical method originated in Greek mystery cults, notably Orphism, as a means of drawing profound truths from the symbolism of the myths surrounding the mystery.[5] Another theory is offered by E. Stein.[6] Allegory arises when there is (1) a reverence for ancient scriptures and writings and (2) progressed philosophical and scientific thinking (3) which has not yet resulted in historical-critical thinking in relation to these traditional documents. Thus by its reading new views into ancient writings, allegory is called forth to spare the old tradition from critical rejection. But it is not at all clear that this apologetic function was the original intention and use of allegory. I. Heinemann notes that there were Greek apologies for the poets which were not allegorical (for instance some of Plutarch's work), and also allegorical works without apologetic purpose, such as Metrodorus'. The same was true in Jewish allegory in antiquity and medieval times, and in Christian and Moslem allegory as well. So Heinemann prefers to see allegory basically as a means of expositing texts, myths, and

---

[2] Cicero describes allegory as a continuous metaphor, *De Orat.* 3.166.

[3] The word is, however, only indirectly attributed to him in secondary sources. See H. von Arnim, *Stoicorum Veterum Fragmenta* I, Leipzig, 1905 ff., p. 526. At any rate, the word was in technical use in the first century B.C. R. Grant, *The Letter and the Spirit*, London, 1957, p. 121, gives several citations.

[4] H. de Lubac, *Histoire et esprit*, Paris, 1950, p. 22 n. 1 cites the first century philosopher Plutarch, *Aud. Poet.* 4, who refers to "ὑπονοίαι now called ἀλληγορίαι".

[5] *Les idées philosophiques et religieuses de Philon d'Alexandrie*, Paris, 1908, pp. 39–41. So W. Nestle, *Vom Mythos zum Logos*, Stuttgart, 1940, p. 129.

[6] *Die allegorische Exegese des Philo aus Alexandreia*, BZAW, 1929, pp. 1–3; so W. Dilthey, *Gesammelte Schriften* V, Leipzig, 1924, p. 322.

pictures which presupposes that the ancient writer or painter had expressed modern ideas, intending his subjects figuratively to mean groups of people, abstract ideas, natural objects, and so on.[7]

At any rate as philosophy and science progressed in Greece, the long-honored poetry of Hesiod and Homer underwent reappraisal. Some thinkers, such as Xenophanes and Pythagoras, affirmed that the poets' crude theologies and mythologies were flatly incompatible with the newer learning, and had to be discarded. But the poems were looked upon by others as symbolic expressions of hidden truths, fully consistent with the best science and philosophy, and became clear after the theological anthropomorphisms and offensive metaphors were allegorically interpreted. The first allegorist of the Homeric poems is generally held to be Theagenes of Rhegium in the late sixth century.[8] Theagenes' work has been lost, but we learn through his successors that he interpreted Homer's anthropomorphic gods as symbols of ethical and unethical behavior, and various natural forces.[9] The Anaxagorus School, the Pythagoreans, Heracliteans, and Cynics subsequently made use of allegorical interpretation. But the most important allegorists after Metrodorus were the Stoics. Of these Zeno, Cleanthes, Chrysippus, Posidonius, and Cornutus stand out. Chrysippus rejected the popular conceptions of the mythical gods, holding that they stood

---

[7] "Zur griechischen Allegoristik", *Mnemosyne*, 1949, pp. 17–18; so also in his *Altjüdische Allegoristik*, Breslau, 1936, pp. 6f., 23f. J. Tate, "Plato and Allegorical Interpretation," CQ, 1929, p. 142f., and "On the History of Allegorism," CQ, 1934, p. 106f., argues similarly.

[8] So H. Hersman, *Studies in Greek Allegorical Interpretation*, Chicago, 1906, p. 10. This view has been challenged by J. Tate, "The Beginnings of Greek Allegory," CR, 1927, p. 214f. He notes that Origen (*c. Celsum* 6.42) remarks that Pherecydes of Syros, born ca. 600 B.C., "interpreted" the words of Zeus to Hera (*Iliad* 15.18) to be the words of God to matter. So the "naturalistic" (φυσικὸς) meaning of Homer for Pherecydes was that matter was in an original confused state, and that God bound it by propositions and put it in order. Pherecydes also interpreted *Iliad* 1.590 in a similar way. Tate's conclusion here and in "Plato and Allegorical Interpretation," CQ, 1929, p. 143f. is therefore that the philosophers and not the rhetorians were the actual originators of the allegory of the Greek myths. But F. Wehrli, *Zur Geschichte der allegorischen Deutung Homers im Altertum*, Basel, 1928, p. 92, regards Metrodorus as the first actual allegorist. Cf. H. Diels, *Fragmente der Vorsokratiker* II, Berlin, 1935, p. 49, fr. 2.

[9] R. Laqueur, RE, VA, c. 1347.

for natural objects or forces.[10] Rhea is earth, Zeus is the all-penetrating Logos.[11] Significantly, Chrysippus decided that some passages of Homer could not be defended even allegorically, and at times disagrees flatly with him.[12]

Some of the Stoic writings included systematic allegorical commentaries on Homer, such as Cornutus' *Nature of the Gods*, and Heraclitus' *Homeric Questions*. About the first century B.C. books such as περὶ τῶν παρ᾽ Ὁμήρῳ νόμων of Dioscurides and περὶ τῆς κα Θ᾽ Ὅμηρον ῥητορικῆς of Telephos, used by Pseudo-Plutarch in *De Vita et Poesi Homeri*, appeared, based upon a systematic allegory of Homer and answering different problems of life.[13] These works resemble in style the commentaries of Philo of Alexandria, *Questions and Answers in Genesis*, and *Exodus*.[14]

2: Alexandrian Jewish Allegory Before Philo

It is noteworthy that the earliest important philosophers of Alexandria took a negative view toward the use of allegory in interpreting the poets.[15] But in the Hellenistic period with the rise of syncretistic tendencies in Alexandria, allegory of stories and myths became highly important in the philosophizing of Egyptian religion. Chaeremon, an Egyptian priest in Alexandria who was also a Stoic philosopher and grammarian, seemingly dependent

---

[10] Wehrli, *op. cit.*, p. 62, notes that Chrysippus claimed the divine could be understood both in mythical and "naturalistic" form. Arnim, *op. cit.*, II fr. 1009, 908, 1976.

[11] *Ibid.* II, 1063.

[12] *Ibid.* II, 925. In this he set himself clearly against the allegorism of the Anaxagorus school. He also differed from the school in using etymology as a tool for hermeneutics. See I. Heinemann, "Zur griechischen Allegoristik," *Mnemosyne*, 1949, p. 9.

[13] Wehrli, *op. cit.*, p. 95.

[14] In *QG* and *QE* Philo uses a well-known literary form of the Greek philosophical schools, ἀπορίαι καὶ λύσεις, in which the λύσις is an exegesis with an apologetic interest. Similarly the fragment of the Jewish Demetrius, *Biblical Chronology;* see P. Dalbert, *Die Theologie der hellenistischen jüdischen Missionsliteratur unter Ausschluss von Philo und Josephus* (*Theologische Forschungen*, Heft 4), Hamburg, 1954, p. 29.

[15] So Eratosthenes ridiculed especially the attempts of the allegorists to ascribe penetrating geographical knowledge to Homer. *Strab.* 1.24, RE, Supp. IV, "Allegorische Dichtererklärung," c. 18.

upon what W. Bousset regarded as the oldest layer of Stoic material in the Hermetic literature, identified the Egyptian gods and their myths with heavenly bodies in their respective movements.[16] The grammarian Philo of Byblos also witnesses to the practice of allegorizing Egyptian mythology.[17] Plutarch's allegory, *On Isis and Osiris*, a later document in the same Egyptian allegorical movement, holds it impiety to understand the myths literally.[18] All this represents a culmination of a Hellenizing of Egyptian religion which had begun during the Ptolemaic period.[19]

The earliest evidences of allegorical method in Alexandrian Judaism are seen in the Septuagint, which was in fairly widespread use by the early part of the third century B.C. Actual allegories in the LXX are not easy to find, but this is to be expected since it is a translation and not a commentary.[20] By its numerous deviations and paraphrases of anthropomorphisms in the Hebrew text, the LXX reflects one of the same motives which was behind the allegorical method as it was applied to Homer's poems, i.e., to remove anthropomorphisms and anthropopathisms ascribed to divinity. It circumscribes Ex. 15.3, "Yahweh is a man of war,"

---

[16] "Die Lehre des Hermes Trismegistus," *Göttingische Gelehrte Anzeigen*, 1914, p. 751f.

[17] Eusebius, *Praep. Evang.* 1.9.25–26.

[18] *De Is. et Os.* 68. 378B.

[19] R. Reitzenstein, *Poimandres, Studien zur griechisch-ägyptischen und frühchristlichen Literatur*, Leipzig, 1904, pp. 1–8. Reitzenstein also notes that Jewish as well as Greek elements entered this meld in the allegorization of Egyptian revelation literature, *ibid.*, p. 158.

[20] A. Gfrörer, *Philo und die alexandrinische Theosophie* I, Stuttgart, 1831, pp. 8–18, and C. Siegfried, *Philo von Alexandria als Ausleger des Alten Testaments*, Jena, 1875, p. 17f., have listed several passages which they feel show allegory, but these are all doubted by P. Heinisch, *Der Einfluss Philos auf die älteste christliche Exegese*, Münster, 1908, pp. 16–17. But I. Heinemann, "Die Allegoristik der hellenistischen Juden ausser Philon," *Mnemosyne*, 1952, pp. 131–132, has convincingly called attention to the LXX rendering of Prov. 2.16–17 as an allegory. The RSV has:

You will be saved from the loose (strange) woman,
from the adventuress (foreign woman) with her smooth words,
who forsakes the companion of her youth
and forgets the convenant of her God.

The LXX takes the woman as a symbol of evil intention, " ... to remove you from the straight way and make you a stranger of righteous purpose. Son, let not evil intention sieze you, which has deserted the teaching of youth, and forgotten the divine covenant."

with "Lord crushing wars;" Numb. 12.8, "and the form of Yahweh shall he behold," with "and the glory of the Lord he saw;" Numb. 11.1, "in the ears of Yahweh," with "before the Lord;" Deut. 33.10, "they shall put incense in thy nostrils," with "they shall lay incense in thine anger;" Ex. 33.14, "and Yahweh repented of the evil," with "and the Lord was moved with compassion."[21] Whether these are due to Greek philosophical influences or the spiritual development within Judaism itself is not certain.[22]

Also of interest for us is the *Wisdom of Solomon's* use of allegorical method in interpreting Biblical episodes and items. The pillar of cloud and fire (Ex. 14.19, etc.) is reinterpreted as a symbol of the Wisdom of God (10.17). Evidently the mysterious figure, "the destroyer" (Ex. 12.23), is allegorized as the Word of God in 18.15. Aaron's robe is taken to mean the world in 18.24.[23]

---

[21] C. Fritsch, *The Anti-Anthropomorphisms of the Greek Pentateuch*, Princeton, 1943, pp. 9–18.

[22] *Ibid.*, p. 3f.
We must recall, however, that Rabbinic Judaism had developed its own reticences with respect to anthropomorphisms attributed to deity. Some of the later targumim show the same dissolving of anthropomorphisms that we have noted in the LXX. So Onkelos continually renders God's hand as his power, his eye as his providence, his feet, back, face as his omnipresence. See S. Maybaum, *Die Anthropomorphien und Anthropopathien bei Onkelos und den spätern Targumim mit besonderer Berücksichtigung der Ausdrücke Memra, Jᵉkara, und Schechintha*, Breslau, 1870, pp. 3–5.
J. Lauterbach has sought to identify two Midrashic exegetical schools, the *Dorsche Reshumot*, and *Dorsche Hamurot*, as Palestinian Jewish allegorists in "The Ancient Jewish Allegorists in the Talmud and Midrash," *Jewish Quarterly Review*, 1910. In *Sifre Deut.* 49 a *Dorsche Reshumot* interpretation is cited for Deut. 11.22, "to walk in all his ways and to cleave unto him." The commentary says that cleaving unto God cannot be taken literally. "How is it possible for a human being to go up to God and cleave unto him?" So to "cleave unto him" really means to imitate him in following his ways. "The original motive of the *Dorsche Reshumot* was to explain away all attributes inconsistent with their idea of a spiritual God. They, therefore, interpreted all anthropomorphic expressions in the scriptures not according to their literal meanings, but in a metaphorical sense," (p. 305). I. Heinemann, *Altjüdische Allegoristik*, pp. 66–68, rejects Lauterbach's thesis, showing numerous Talmudic and Midrashic passages attributed to those schools containing no allegory. But for our purposes it is enough to note these efforts in normative Judaism to reinterpret Biblical anthropomorphisms.

[23] The high priest's garments were consistently allegorized by Philo to refer to the cosmos; cf. *Mig.* 103; *Fug.* 110; *Som.* I 215; Josephus, *Ant.* III 184, and above pp. 58 ff.

16

Apparently the first Alexandrian Jewish philosopher to utilize allegorical exegesis was the second century B.C. writer Aristobulus who wrote an extensive series of works on the Mosaic laws, according to Clement of Alexandria's allusion (*Strom.* 5.14.97). Two passages from his work are preserved for us in Eusebius' *Praep. Evang.* 8.10, and 13.12. From these sources we learn that Aristobulus was trying to prove through allegorical method that the best Greek philosophers and poets were dependent upon a pre-Septuagint translation of Moses' books for their leading ideas.[24] Since the only allegories of Aristobulus that have come down to us have to do with anthropomorphisms attributed to God in the Holy Scripture, from what we have seen in this respect in the LXX, the resolving of anthropomorphisms was evidently one of the primary reasons for the rise of this hermeneutics in Alexandrian Judaism.[25]

The next source in the Alexandrian Jewish exegesis leading up to Philo is *The Letter of Aristeas*. A date of about 100–150 B.C. is now generally given to the letter.[26] The writer praises the Jewish high priest Eleazar for his allegorical apology on the laws of the Pentateuch against the charges that the Scriptures contained mythology (167–170). Important for our consideration is the way the high priest defends the dietary laws of Moses. The legislation forbidding the eating of birds of prey, he says, must be interpreted "spiritually" ($\varkappa\alpha\tau\grave{\alpha}\ \varphi\upsilon\chi\grave{\eta}\nu$, 147), and teaches not to rob anything,

---

I. Heinemann, "Die Allegoristik der hellenistischen Juden ausser Philon," *Mnemosyne*, 1952, p. 137, denies that there is allegory in *Wisdom* and calls this treatment symbolic interpretation. But I do not distinguish symbolic from allegorical interpretation. For one thing, Philo used the words "symbolically" and "allegorically" interchangeably; as does the allegorist Plutarch; cf. *Prob.* 82; *Cont.* 78; *De Is.* 363 F. Both words refer to the hidden meaning of the text.

[24] The Hellenistic Jewish historian Artapanus argued similarly, claiming that Abraham taught the Pharoah of Egypt astrology, and that Moses, known to the Greeks as Musaeus, gave the Egyptians their philosophy and was called Hermes by the priests; Eusebius, *Praep. Evang.* 9.18, 9.27.3–6. *Aristeas* 314 also refers to a pre-LXX Greek translation.

[25] Aristobulus points out the figurative meaning of the anthropomorphic references to God's voice, hands, arm, face, feet, and descending and walking. God's standing designates the unchangeable character of his works and the firm order of the world; Eusebius *Praep. Evang.* 10.1–17.

[26] P. Wendland, JE II, p. 93; Moses Hadas, *Aristeas to Philocrates*, New York, 1951, p. 17.

nor oppress anyone. The laws concerning animals "parting the hoof," and with "cloven hoof," the priest interprets as symbols enjoining discrimination concerning good and evil, and separation from evil-doing (150–152). The animals "chewing the cud" are taken as symbols of memory, instructing us to remember what the Lord has done for us (153–163).[27] By the same symbolic treatment, he defends the legislation proscribing eating weasel and mice against the charge that these are arbitrary laws (161–168). Such allegorizing of the laws plays an important part in Philo's hermeneutics.[28]

These pre-Philonic sources suggest the forming of a tradition of Jewish allegorical exegesis in Alexandria. We see that one task of this exegesis at least was the rational defence of the Scriptures using allegory to show the harmony between Scripture and philosophy, as in the efforts of Aristobulus and *The Letter of Aristeas*.[29] Furthermore, as we turn to Philo himself, we note that many of his allegorical renderings of Biblical passages are not original to him, having been received by him from older Jewish sources. He frequently introduces allegorical material with certain formulas indicating his dependence upon other allegorical exegetes. Such are formulas as $\mathring{\eta}\varkappa o\upsilon\sigma\alpha$, "I have heard some natural philosophers who took the passage allegorically" (*Abr.* 99; cf. *Jos.* 151), or "$\tau\iota\nu\acute{\epsilon}\varsigma\ \varphi\alpha\sigma\iota\nu$" (*Her.* 280; *Mos.* II 98; *QG* I 8; III 13), or such phrases as "But to those who are accustomed to turn literal facts into allegory..." (*Spec.* II 147; *QE* II 71; *Plant.* 74).[30] He refers to his allegorical predecessors as "interpreters of the holy scriptures" (*Spec.* II 159), some of whose allegories he takes up (*Mut.* 141; *QG* I 10; *Plant.* 52), and others he rejects (*LA* I 59; *QG* II 11; I 8).

---

[27] Philo gives this interpretation of the cloven hoof in *Spec.* IV 108, and the same explanation of the chewing of the cud in *Agr.* 131–145; see below pp. 50 ff.

[28] Compare the above exposition with Philo's commentary on the dietary law permitting the eating of locusts in Lev. 11.22, *Opif.* 163. Philo thinks this is actually a praise of the reptile he calls a "snake-fighter", which in turn is a symbol of one who exercises self-control, fighting against pleasure, symbolized by the serpent.

[29] I. Heinemann, *Altjüdische Allegoristik*, p. 70, who denies that the sole motive for allegory in Hellenistic Judaism was apologetic, an assertion he also holds in connection with Greek allegory (see above p. 12), admits that apologetics was one motive.

[30] E. Bréhier, *op. cit.*, p. 55 f.

18

Philo regards allegory as a mystery into which one must be initiated, and designates non-allegorical exegetes as "those who are uninitiated in allegory and the nature-truth which loves to conceal its meaning" (*Fug.* 179). He even claims that the Jews who do not follow his hermeneutics have in effect corrupted their religion into superstition (*Cher.* 42; *Abr.* 200; *Plant.* 36). By Philo's time an earlier inclination toward allegorizing had become a thorough-going school of Jewish exegesis whose adherents regarded themselves, in contrast with the rest of Judaism, as having the authentic method for uncovering the essential message of Scripture.

3: Philo's Place in the Allegorical Tradition

Philo Judaeus was undoubtedly a highly respected man in Alexandrian Judaism and from a wealthy family.[31] When refusal to erect images to the emperor cult in their synagogues brought severe persecution to Alexandrian Jews, Philo was selected to head a delegation of Jews to request exemption from emperor cult worship from Emperor Gaius for his co-religionists in his city during the fall of 39 A.D. Not much was accomplished by this delegation, but after Gaius was murdered, Emperor Claudius granted the Alexandrian Jews their request.[32]

From the first sentence of *On the Embassy to Gaius* we learn that Philo was an old man when he wrote the treatise sometime during the reign of Emperor Claudius. So a likely estimate of his lifespan would be between 20 B.C. and 50 A.D. He remarks that he was once on the coast of Syria on his way to the temple in Jerusalem to offer prayers and sacrifices (*Prov.* II 64). This and his detailed descriptions of the Essene sect (*Prob.* 75–91; *Apo.* 11.1–18) show that he must have spent considerable time in Palestine and had personal contact with Palestinian Judaism. His Jewish and Greek learning plus his reliance on the Jewish allegorical tradition in Alexandria prepared him for his voluminous expository work on the sacred scriptures. But we must not think of Philo as a scholastic given over exclusively to religious reflection. He recalls

---

[31] Josephus, *Ant.* 18.259.

[32] *Ibid.*, 19. The text of Claudius' letter to Alexandria to this effect can be seen in H. Bell's *Jews and Christians in Egypt*, British Museum, 1924.

once with nostalgia how in his earlier days he was able to give undivided attention to philosophical studies, only to have this life interrupted by civic responsibilities and public administration (*Spec.* II 1–3; cf. *Fug.* 35–36). A related fact reported by Josephus is that Philo's brother Alexander Lysimachus was Arabach of Alexandria, that is, controller of customs, during the time of Tiberius and Gaius.[33]

Philo's allegorical method unmistakably places him in the long line of Greek and Hellenistic allegorical tradition whose chief exponents were the Stoics. In perfect Stoic fashion Philo even hands down a de-anthropomorphized allegory of the story in Hesiod, *Theog.* 50f., according to which Zeus lay nine nights with Mnemosyne, who subsequently bore the Nine Muses. According to the Judaized version Philo had heard, Mnemosyne is identified with one of the metaphysical powers of God, Memory, from which the Muses and hymnody sprang.[34] Philo, like the Greek interpreters, refers often to the allegorical sense as the "natural" or "scientific" meaning (*Abr.* 99; *Som.* I 120; *Post.* 7). Historically the equation of the φυσικὸς sense with the allegorical one grew out of the assertion that the Greek poets were really writing their views about natural science in the dress of metaphor. In fact Philo's continual use of the technical terminology used by the Greek allegorists links him unequivocally with the same hermeneutical method of secular philosophy and rhetoric. Some of these technical terms are: αἴνιγμα, "riddle" (*Som.* II 3, 4; *LA* III 226, 231), αἰνίσσεσθαι, "to mean figuratively" (*Post.* 18; *Det.* 155, 178), δεῖγμα and ὑπόδειγμα, "example" (*Post.* 122; *Conf.* 64; *Sac.* 120, 139; *Opif.* 157), ᾿εξηγησις, "exposition" (*Cont.* 78; *Spec.* II 159), ἑρμηνεία, "interpretation" (*Mos.* II 191; *Mig.* 35), θεωρία, "view" (*Spec.* II 29), μηνύειν, "to indicate" (*Opif.* 77; *Mos.* I

---

[33] *Ant.* 18.259, 159; 19.276; 20.100; see H. Box, *Philonis Alexandrini in Flaccum*, xxxii, Oxford, 1939.

[34] *Plant.* 127–129; see also Colson's note *ad loc.* Brehier, *op. cit.*, p. 38 n. 1, parallels this allegory with Cornutus' treatment of it. Philo also reinterprets the mythical Hades not as a place but as an accursed life lived in evil; *Cong.* 57; *Her.* 45. The strength of Mars is a symbol of manliness (*Legat.* 112), Hera is air, Hephaestus is fire, Apollo is the sun, Artemis is the moon, Aphrodite is the morning-star, and Hermes is the glitterer (*Dec.* 54; *Cont.* 3). For Stoic parallels see P. Wendland, *Philos Schrift über die Vorsehung*, Berlin, 1892, p. 61 n. 2.

217; *Dec.* 101), σύμβολον, "symbol" (*Spec.* III 178; *Sac.* 112; *Mut.* 253), παράδειγμα, "model" or "pattern" (*Mos.* I 158; *Cher.* 14), σημαίνειν, "to signify" (*Cong.* 155; *Post.* 154; *Plant.* 151), ὑπονοία, "deeper sense" (*Praem.* 65; *Jos.* 28), τροπικῶς, "figuratively" (LA I 45).[35]

From Philo's descriptions we learn that there were parties of Jews in Alexandria which had rejected this Greek allegorical method as applied to Biblical interpretation. Throughout his writings he is in continual debate with these literalists who see only τὸ ῥητόν, the letter of the text. They fail to see, or refuse to see, a deeper, allegorical sense. Such literalists were of three kinds. First, there were the ones who were just slow-witted, who out of ignorance missed the allegorical meaning entirely (*Fug.* 179; *Det.* 22; *Som.* I 39). Second, there were the stubborn conservatives, rigid and resentful toward any change of view who clung defiantly to their literalism (*Som.* II 301).[36] Philo's polemic against the Alexandrian literalists of the first two types is that their method lands them in impossible difficulties and even forces them to make deductions from Scripture which are tantamount to gross ungodliness, such as concluding that God can and does repent (*Immut.* 21; cf. also *Mig.* 45, 46). Furthermore, literal interpretation never exhausts the meaning of the text. It is only by allegorical hermeneutics that one can appreciate why Scripture sometimes uses the term "husbandman" and elsewhere "soil-worker," and also why it uses "shepherd" and in another passage "cattle-rearer."[37] A third group were Jewish apostates who vilified the scriptures, seeing nothing but the literal sense, and because they refused to accept it as true, rejected the Bible altogether (*Conf.* 2, 6–8; *Agr.* 157; *Ebr.* 65; *Mut.* 61, 62). Helicon, who claimed to have been nurtured in Judaism, and subsequently ridiculed it, would belong to this group (*Legat.* 168–170).[38]

Once the method of allegorizing the Torah which we noted first in *The Letter of Aristeas* was introduced, it became inevitable that

---

[35] For a further discussion on most of these terms and their instances in secular literature, see R. Grant, *op.* cit., pp. 120–145.

[36] M. Shroyer, "Alexandrian Jewish Literalists," JBL, 1936, p. 273.

[37] *Agr.* 26–29, 20–21, 39–42, 57; H. Wolfson, *Philo, Foundations of Religious Philosophy in Judaism, Christianity, and Islam* I, Cambridge, Mass., 1947, p. 61.

[38] M. Shroyer, *op. cit.*, pp. 273–281.

this symbolic interpretation would be driven by some to the exclusion of the literal observance of the laws. Philo raises his objections to just such a group of extreme allegorists in Alexandria. He agrees with this group that the symbolic teaching of the observance of the Sabbath is to remind us of God's eternal activity and our meager efforts in comparison with it, that holy festivals are symbols of the soul's gladness and thankfulness to God, and that circumcision represents the cutting away of pleasure and passions; but these observances ought not to be ignored on that account. For in heeding the letter of these laws we become more clearly instructed as to the symbolic meaning behind them. Also because we live in community we must obey the literal laws, if not for the acquisition of perfect virtue, at least for civic virtue (*Mig.* 91–93; *Sac.* 78).[39] So Philo occupied a middle position in Alexandrian Judaism, defending the legitimacy of allegory against its literalist objectors as an indispensable apologetic and hermeneutical tool on the one hand, and on the other hand pleaing for respect of the literal meaning of Scripture against the left-wing allegorists.

4: Philo's Vindication of Allegory

Because of the controversial place of allegory, Philo found it necessary at the same time to apologize for the scriptures and for his method of apology. Philo's defence of his principles of interpretation is that the Bible all but openly says that we dare not interpret it literally, for it is only too plain that the literal meaning of Scripture does not do justice to the depth of the Bible, and often implies absurdities. As we mentioned above, Philo urged the allegorical sense be sought whenever something impious, such as anthropomorphic descriptions, are attributed to God. Gen. 11.5,

---

[39] J. Lauterbach, *op. cit.*, p. 329 n. 32, notes that Rabbinic Judaism also saw the danger in allegorical interpretation in that the laws could be so interpreted that none of them needed to be literally observed. Therefore the allegorical method of *rashum* or *mashal* was forbidden to be applied to any scripture passages containing commandments and laws; cf. rule 26 of the thirty-two rules of Haggadic interpretation of R. Eliezer b. R. Jose Hagelili, and I. Heinemann, *Altjüdische Allegoristik*, p. 37. This prohibition, however, was not observed. J. Bónsirven, "Exégèse allégorique chez les rabbins tannaites," *Recherches de science religieuse*, 1933, pp. 522–524, cites several cases of allegorical treatment of Biblical legislation.

"The Lord came down to see the city and the tower," is an anthropomorphic impiety if taken literally, for God transcends the universe itself, and at the same time cannot be thought of as leaving any part of the universe without his presence. Surely the passage must be understood figuratively (*Conf.* 134f.) Similarly God's reportedly planting a garden in Gen. 2.8 must not be understood literally, but ought to be taken as God's planting heavenly virtue in human kind (*LA* I 43–46).

Philo is fond of quoting emphatically Numb. 23.19, "God is not as man" (*Sac.* 94; *Immut.* 53; *Conf.* 98; *Mig.* 113; *Som.* I 237; *QG* I 55, II 54). Now interpreting Biblical anthropomorphisms symbolically was a general characteristic of Late-Judaism, as we have seen. But Philo went beyond normative Judaism in these concerns and had another purpose in wanting to avert anthropomorphisms than just the reverence for the Biblical transcendence of God. He warns what the consequences are of thinking of God in human terms. If human organs are attributed to God, then the functions of those organs also go with them, for Nature "has not made idle superfluities, but aids to the weaknesses of those furnished with them" (*Post.* 4). So such bodily descriptions of God are $ἀσεβῶν$ $αὗται$ $μυθυποιίαι$ $λόγῳ$ $μεν$ $ἀνθρωπόμορφον$ $ἔργῳ$ $δὲ$ $ἀνθρωποπαθὲς$ $εἰσαγόντων$ $τὸ$ $θεῖον$ (*Immut.* 59). Here $λόγῳ$ and $ἔργῳ$ standing in contrast to each other give the sentence the force of: "These are myth-makings of the impious who under the pretext of representing the deity in human terms, in actual practice depict him as having human passions." The same contrast between $λόγος$ and $ἔργον$ is present in *Sac.* 95: "We shun indeed in words the monstrosity of saying that God is of human form, but in actual fact we accept the impious thought that he is of human passions." In *Post.* 4 he says, "Anthropopathism follows anthropomorphism inevitably." We may understand, then, that Philo's real concern was to safeguard the serene beatific happiness of God, untroubled by the passions of mortal flesh, which issue inevitably from bodily organs. If such are ever attributed to God, he says: "These things are out of harmony with the blessedness and happiness of the First Cause—lawless inventions of men who represent him anthropomorphically and even ($ἔτι$ $δὲ$ $καί$) anthropopathically . . ." (*Plant.* 35).

C. Siegfried assembled other circumstances in which literal descriptions should give way to allegorical ones in attempting to reconstruct what Philo called the "canons of allegory" (*Som.* I 73; *Spec.* I 287), or "laws of allegory" (*Abr.* 68).[40] When the text presents insoluble difficulty, or contains no sense, or a contradiction, or something inadmissible or unworthy of Scripture, the literal meaning should be given up for the allegorical one. Gen. 4.15 states that anyone who murders Cain shall unloose seven punishments, but this cannot be taken literally because it is completely unclear as to what the seven are, or how they are punishable, or how they are loosed (*Det.* 167). Gen. 11.5 states that the Lord came down to see the city and tower which the men had already built, a literal contradiction with 11.6 which states that "they have begun to do this" (*Conf.* 152). Ps. 46.4, "The strong current of the river makes glad the city of God," cannot be meant literally because the literal Jerusalem is far from rivers and seas (*Som.* II 246). Gen. 9.25, according to which Canaan, not Ham, is cursed, is certainly literally improper since Ham and not his offspring had committed the sin (*Sob.* 31–34).

Philo laid down the principle that upon careful search nothing base or unworthy of the oracles of God could be found in them, which was important for some of his commentary on O.T. legislation (*Det.* 13). To the legislation

> If ever you take your neighbor's garment in pledge, you shall restore it to him before the sun goes down; for that is his only covering, it is his mantle for his body. (Ex. 22.26f.)

Philo offers several objections to literal interpretation, including the *argumentum ad absurdum*, should God who is creator and ruler of the universe concern himself over such a trifling matter as the return of garments (*Som.* I 92–94)?[41]

Also unworthy of sacred scripture was anything Philo thought was "mythical" in character. G. Delling determined the meaning of the word "myth" for Philo as "a fictitious tale, a false explanation of something enigmatic, usually belonging to pre-

---

[40] *Op. cit.*, pp. 166ff.

[41] Cf. *Fug.* 107–112. In the Talmud there is a protest against this allegorizing of laws which deal with seeming trivialities. In reference to Deut. 22.6, *Berakot* 33a reads, "Whoever says, 'Do God's mercies extend to the bird's nest? Can God concern himself with such trivial things?' is to be silenced". J. Lauterbach, *op. cit.*, p. 530. Note the similarity with Paul's treatment of Deut. 25.4 in 1 Cor. 9.8–10.

history, and always at bottom dealing with the sphere of the religious".[42] Philo charges that the Stoic doctrine of world conflagration is mythical (*Her.* 228),[43] and in the same way he rejects Greek folklore (*Dec.* 55; *Aet.* 57–58; *Praem.* 8, 9), claiming that Moses avoids such falsities (*Opif.* 2).[44] Any passage in Moses which at the literal level appears mythical, such as the creation of woman from Adam's rib (*LA* II 19), or the serpent's speaking with a human voice (*Agr.* 96f.), can only be rightly understood when the mythical elements are symbolically reinterpreted.[45]

Sometimes the symbolic expression of the Bible itself demands that we take the allegorical meaning instead of the literal one. When Gen. 2.9 speaks of the tree of knowledge and the tree of life, this can only be interpreted symbolically, since no such trees have ever actually appeared (*Plant.* 36–39; *Opif.* 154).[46]

---

[42] "Wunder-Allegorie-Mythus bei Philon von Alexandreia," *Gottes ist der Orient, Festschrift für O. Eissfeldt*, Berlin, 1959, p. 56. Cf. *Mut.* 152; *Som.* I 171; *Mos.* II 253.

[43] This doctrine was given up, however, by one Stoic, Panaetius, in his critique of Carneades, declaring the world to be eternel. See E. Turowski, *Die Widerspiegelung des stoischen Systems bei Philon von Alexandreia*, Borna, Leipzig, 1927, pp. v, 59.

[44] Philo thus joins both the Jewish and the Greek-Hellenistic philosophical condemnation of mythology. G. Staehlin, TWNT IV, p. 777, W. Nestle, *op. cit., passim.*

[45] Celsus, ἀληθὴς λόγος IV 36, is apparently dependent upon Philo at *LA* II 19 and elsewhere, continuing Philo's accusation of mythology. Unlike Philo, however, he rejects any allegorical reinterpretation in attempting to discredit the Bible; E. Stein, *Alttestamentliche Bibelkritik in der späthellenistischen Literatur*, Lwow, 1935, p. 45f.

[46] J. Lauterbach, *op. cit.*, p. 310, notes a Midrashic application of this same principle, *Mekilta* d. r. Simeaon, 72, and *B. Baba Kamma* 82a. With regard to the symbolism of water in Ex. 15.22, the exegesis notes its obvious symbolic reference to religious instruction in Is. 55.1.

In addition to these three general cases in which the literal intention is displaced by the allegorical one, Siegfried reconstructed several other "canons of allegory" of a second type for cases when the literal sense was not excluded but indicated an allegorical meaning above and beyond the literal one. These so-called "canons" have been faithfully copied by writers ever since as representing basic hermeneutical principles of Philo (for instance Heinisch, *op. cit.*, pp. 70–87, Lauterbach, *op. cit., passim*). Several of the "canons" of this type are simply sub-divisions or modifications of the first three principles laid down above. Rule 1, that a deeper meaning is indicated whenever a doubled expression occurs, or 2, whenever an apparently superficial expression appears, or 3, whenever there is a repetition of some matter previously

The question then was raised, either by some of Philo's con-
temporaries, or in his own mind, why does the Bible speak about
God in terms that can be so easily misconstrued (*Immut.* 60).
If Moses who wrote, "God is not as man" (Numb. 23.19), were
asked how then he could write that God will bear you "as a man"
bears his son (Deut. 1.31; *Sac.* 91–101), or why he speaks of God's
arming himself for war, he would answer that as lawgiver it was
his task to try to benefit everyone who reads his works. The wise
and gifted people will see at once that God cannot be described
by the attributes of any created being and take to heart the teaching
"God is not as man." But by condescension to slow-witted people
in no way able to contemplate the uncreated God except through
human terms, such human feelings as wrath and so on are attri-

---

said and already known, are all applications of the principle according to
which whenever the text contains no sense, the allegorical meaning is to be
sought. The remaining eighteen rules which Siegfried listed on close examin-
ation do not appear to describe what Philo felt were clear references to an
allegorical sense of Scripture, but rather amount to observations of exegetical
mechanics which Philo often applied in the process of allegory. Cf. rule 8,
"A specific allegorical meaning can be derived from individual parts of a
word;" rule 11, "It is also permissible through slight changes within a word
to disclose a new meaning" (pp. 174–326).

Siegfried seems to have thought that he was restoring a very carefully
worked out set of hermeneutical principles which guided Philo's thinking
throughout his exegetical work, and which made up an elaborate system for
allegorical interpretation. "Nothing is more incorrect than the assertion,"
he says, that Philo "proceeds arbitrarily" (p. 165). That the so-called "canons
of allegory" which Philo occasionally refers to but never specifies nor enumerates, formed no such exegetical system like the *middoth* of Rabbi Hillel
guiding the interpretation according to established rules is clearly evident
from the way Philo can interpret a given passage first one way and then
another; see E. Stein, *Die allegorische Exegese des Philo aus Alexandreia*,
p. 49, and below, pp. 32 ff.

The principles which we have accepted from Siegfried as conditions for
the exclusion of the literal meaning of the text ought to be thought of as
Philo's apology for allegory to the Jews who refused to accept it. There is
no reason to connect these principles with what Philo mentioned as the
"canons" or "laws" of allegory. E. Bréhier, *op. cit.*, p. 57 n. 1, is probably
right in regarding these phrases as terms meant for the changing of something
literal and sense-perceptible into something allegorical and intelligible. Philo
does not, like the rabbis, wait for the text to present obstacles to literal interpretation, or suggestions at a hidden meaning before he allegorizes it. Cf.
Det. 103; 114.

buted to him, for only in this way can fools be admonished to fear him (*Immut.* 60–68).[47]

Having justified his disputed hermeneutics within the premises of the sacred text itself at least to his own satisfaction and to that of like-minded exegetes, Philo felt free to apply the method at will. He was thus equipped to argue the case for Biblical truth before those apostate Jews whose Hellenistic sophistication had caused them to reject it as intellectually untenable (*Praem.* 152, 162), showing that the best Greek philosophy coincided with and even plagiarized the hidden meaning of Scripture.[48] Philo's Biblical apologetic also served to attract proselytes to Judaism (*Praem.* 152).

Aside from its apologetic function, allegory also helped Philo to read his peculiar mystical interpretation of Judaism into the books of the O.T. In *Cher.* 35–39 an allegory on Balaam and his ass is turned to an admonition to see in misfortune not chance but providence at work. This is an example of yet another use of allegory, a parenetic or homiletic use which Philo frequently employed to yield up moral lessons from the Bible for Jewish readers. E. Stein attests to the importance of the homiletic use of allegory for its development in the Palestinian Midrash as well.[49]

---

[47] In *Som.* I 237 Philo refers to Numb. 23.19 as the way πρὸς τὸ ἀληθές and to Deut. 8.5, "as a man disciplines his son the Lord, your God disciplines you," as the way πρὸς τὰς δόξας, pointing these out as the two ways of expression in the Torah, graded for higher and lower mental types respectively. Antisthenes and Zeno had both distinguished between the exegesis κατὰ ἀλήθειαν and exegesis κατὰ δόξαν. Philo has preserved this Stoic dichotomy and terminology; J. Pépin, *Mythe et allegorie*, Paris, 1958, p. 238. This didactic explanation of Biblical anthropomorphisms was also known to Rabbinic Judaism. With reference to anthropomorphic expressions in Amos 3.8 and Ezek. 43.2, *Mekilta, Bahodesh*, 4, F, p. 65a, explains that God is described in creaturely terms in order that they may sink into men's ears, that is, to assist the understanding; H. Wolfson, *op. cit.*, I, p. 135.

[48] *Her.* 214; *Prob.* 57; *Mut.* 167–168; *Mig.* 128; *QG* III 5, IV 152; II 6; *Spec.* IV 61. During Philo's time Egyptian religious philosophers were claiming that Greek philosophy had borrowed from the Egyptians; E. Zeller, *Die Philosophie der Griechen* I, Leipzig, 1903, p. 22 n. 2.

[49] *Alttestamentliche Bibelkritik in der späthellenistischen Literatur*, p. 40. Recall the parenetic character of the LXX allegory of Prov. 2.16–17 which we noted above, p. 6f. n. 20.

CHAPTER II

Uncovering the Hidden Meaning

1: The Two-Level View of Scripture

As it was earlier mentioned, Philo protested against the left-wing allegorists who rejected the literal meaning of the Biblical laws. He did not deny that Scripture has a literal and historical meaning. A. Gfrörer wrote that Philo had taken some passages of scripture *only* literally.[1] Still Philo himself says, "All or most of the law-book is an allegory" (*Jos.* 28). At any rate, Philo generally sees the Scripture possessing two meanings side by side, literal and allegorical. His understanding of the twin meanings of Scripture which stand one on top the other is most apparent in his works, *Questions and Answers on Genesis*, and *Exodus*. Here he regularly exposits the literal sense of the text and afterwards the allegorical one, changing from one level to the other with his standard formula, "This is the literal meaning. But as for the deeper meaning..." He praises Moses' intention in Gen. 2.19 saying, "Both the tropic (allegorical) and the literal interpretation are things worthy of amazement" (*LA* II 14; cf. *Som.* I 120f.). The Lord's words to Aaron in Lev. 10.8–10 proscribing wine and strong drink before going to the altar are "amazing" both literally and allegorically, since men should have full control of themselves in prayer on the one hand, and on the other hand folly, symbolized by wine, can never attain to virtue, the altar (*Ebr.* 127–139).

After first expositing the literal meaning of a text, Philo often introduces the allegorical one with various phrases such as: τὰ νοητὰ (*Abr.* 217), ἀσώματα καὶ γυμνὰ πράγματα (*ibid.* 236), τὰ ἐν ὑπονοίαις (*Jos.* 28), ἡ τροπικὴ ἀπόδοσις (*LA* II 14), ἡ τροπικωτέρα ἀπόδοσις (*Jos.* 125), ἡ δι᾿ ὑπονοιῶν ἀπόδοσις (*Abr.* 88), ἡ ἐν ἀλληγορίᾳ θεωρία (*Abr.* 131), ὁ τρόπος ἀλληγορίας (*Dec.* 1), ἡ ἐν ἀποκρύφῳ

---

[1] *Op. cit.* I, p. 86.

καὶ πρὸς ὀλίγους ἀπόδοσις (*Abr*. 147).[2] Pépin[3] supposes it was Philo's original contribution to allegorical exegesis to recognize the two layers of meaning. But Wehrli[4] recalls that Chrysippus held that divinity could be understood both mythically (that is, corresponding to the literal text of the poems) and "naturally", i.e., allegorically.

Nevertheless except in his tracts in which he is specifically concerned with relating Biblical history, the literal sense is definitely of lesser importance to Philo than the deeper one. He admits "perhaps" there was an historical Samuel, but his main interest is in the allegorical Samuel, in the mind which rejoices in the worship and serving of God only (*Ebr*. 144). Those who remain with the first level of Scripture alone are "uncritical" (*Immut*. 21; *Her*. 91) and superficial. But it is not as if the literal level of the text is unrelated to the allegorial one. The two are analogous to body and soul. As we must care for the body since it houses the soul, so we must pay attention to the letter of the text which contains within it the more important deeper meaning (*Mig*. 93). The bodily form of the literal text points the way to the inward soul characteristics (τρόπους ψυχῆς) resembling through outward manifestations the spiritual qualities, modes, and relationships within (*Abr*. 131ff, 147). Or another analogy between the two meanings is that of shadow and reality. The words of the text, as it were, are the shadows cast by the allegorical substance beneath and behind them (*Conf*. 190).

The latter dichotomy is in agreement with Philo's general Platonic epistemology which he has transferred to his view of Scripture. Commenting on Gen. 28.17 where Jacob says, "This is none other than the house of God, and this is the gate of heaven," he takes the "house of God" to mean the visible world and as such is the "gate of" the real "heaven." In this way it stands in

---

[2] C. Siegfried, *op. cit.*, p. 164.

[3] *Op. cit.*, p. 232.

[4] See above, p. 14 n. 10. Illustrations of a two-layer understanding of scripture occur in Rabbinic Judaism as well. For instance *Mekhilta* comments on Ex. 15.1, "Then sang Moses," first as referring to the event related in the Pentateuch, then regarded the verse as saying, "Then Moses will sing," and took it as a reference to the last days and as a proof for the resurrection of the dead; D. Daube, "Alexandrian Methods of Interpretation and the Rabbis," *Festschrift Hans Lewald*, Basel, 1953, p. 38 n. 59.

the relationship of "shadow" to reality, being the outwardly perceptible manifestation of a heavenly dimension beyond and behind it. It is only through the gate that one can enter the city. We cannot come to a knowledge of the non-perceptible ideal world except through the perceptible world, the gate to the intelligible world. To attain to knowledge of an incorporeal essence we must take its material counterpart as our starting point, passing then from the earthly copy to the eternal reality beyond it (*Som*. I 185–188). Following this theory of knowledge, which is not the only theory of knowledge to be found in Philo but the one which concerns us here,[5] we must begin with the shadow-like words of the scripture and then pass beyond them to the ideas which lie on the allegorical level from which they are projected.[6]

We could at the same time think of Philo's two level view of scripture as conditioned by his world view. The visible world is structured according to an ideal invisible world which transcends it. When God created the visible world,

> He first fully formed the intelligible world, in order that He might have use of a pattern wholly God-like and incorporeal in producing the material world, as a later creation, the very image of an earlier one, to embrace in itself objects of perception of as many kinds as the other contained objects of intelligence (*Opif*. 16).

It was this world of incorporeal paradigmatic essences of ideas which Moses was shown on the mountain top in Ex. 26.30 (*QE* II 90). Philo elsewhere describes this world as a noumenal world, accessible to the mind, just as the phenomenal world is perceived

---

[5] Wolfson, *op. cit.*, II, pp. 5–11, gives others which he tries to combine into a general theory.

[6] Philo's shadow-reality frame of epistemological thinking obtains throughout his psychological theory. If this schema is remembered one can better understand his often derogatory discussion of "speech". Speech as expression is but the shadow of real thought so that verbal expression is merely a copy of the latter. Hence the need to go beyond speech, i.e., verbal expression, and to penetrate to naked ideas themselves (*Mig*. 12). He further explains the relatively inferior place of literal language, both oral and written, in *Mut*. 62–65. Recalling that God assigned to Adam the task of giving names to the animals (Gen. 2.19), Philo concludes that whenever God uses human words and names we must think of them as signs which point beyond themselves. Consequently only through allegorical interpretation can the thoughts intended in words and names, such as Sarah and Abraham, be properly understood.

by the senses (*Her.* 111). This Platonic world of ideas perceptible only by the mind is the world of which Moses writes in allegory, having seen it revealed on the mountain, or having experienced it after pitching his tent outside the camp (*Gig.* 54). Therefore Philo can refer to allegorical truths as ἐν τοῖς κατὰ διάνοιαν (*Agr.* 27), or as τὸ πρὸς διάνοιαν (as R. Marcus continually renders the Armenian into what was probably the original Greek throughout *Questions and Answers in Genesis* and *Exodus*), since man's διάνοια is "an instrument for knowing God, heavenly things, and heavenly wisdom."[7] Having concluded an exposition of the literal text, Philo proceeds to the allegorical meaning of it saying, "Spoken words contain symbols of things apprehended by the διάνοια only" (*Abr.* 119; cf. *Spec.* I 214). Thus the literal meaning corresponds to the sensible everyday world of phenomena and deals with objects, persons, events, and things of the objective world in general. On the other hand, the allegorical meaning lying beyond the literal treats of timeless ideas such as the structure of the creation, the ethical life, and the soul's journey from corporeality to incorporeality.[8]

So Philo says that we can understand the migration of Abraham from Chaldea to Canaan, for instance, two ways:

> The migrations as set forth by the literal text of the scriptures are made by a man of wisdom, but according to the laws of allegory by a virtue-loving soul in its search for the true God (*Abr.* 68, cf. 88).

The story of Abraham is on the literal level the history of a righteous patriarch. But the story of Abraham on the allegorical level is the history of the soul which turns away from the sensible order to the contemplation of the invisible and intelligible order (*Abr.* 88; cf. *Praem.* 61–65). The allegorical story of the soul is actually descriptive of our experience, our existence, not just that of the Biblical worthies. God leads "us" out of Egypt, that is, bodily passions; "we" encamp at Marah when fleshly appetites drag

---

[7] So H. Leisegang defines the word, *Philonis Alexandrini Opera quae Supersunt* VII/I, Berlin, 1926, p. 182.

[8] Although J. Tate, "On the History of Allegorism," CQ, 1934, p. 111, does not mention Philo in this context, he notes that the presuppositions of Neo-Platonic interpretation of the myths is that the myths in some measure express the divine truth in the same way that the visible world is an expression of the invisible reality.

"us" down, although "we" wish to be free of them, so that "we" come to feel that the struggle is bitter and plan to return to Egypt and give up after all. But God thrusts into "our" soul the sweetening tree like syrup which produces a love of labor instead of hatred of labor (*Post.* 155–157). Through Philo's hermeneutics the people of Israel's experiences are made contemporary with our own.[9]

One feature of Philo's exegesis which has interested many scholars is the way in which he can interpret a text or character first one way and then another often contradicting himself completely. Thus Joseph is first taken as a symbol of the many-sided pride of life, and then as a symbol for aesthetic value (*Conf.* 72). God's words concerning mind, the offspring of Eve, to pleasure, the serpent, "He shall watch thy head, and thou shalt watch his heel" (Gen. 3.15), have two allegorical meanings: If the mind is good it will watch for pleasure to destroy it; if the mind is foolish, it will watch for pleasure to delight in it (*LA* III 188–189). Esau who threatens to kill Jacob in Gen. 27.42–45 is first taken to mean the worst part of the soul which threatens to overthrow the better part, and then as the base propounder of immoral doctrines (*Fug.* 24, 25).

How is it that Philo so easily reverses and apparently contradicts himself? In *LA* II 12–13 Philo recalls that the Genesis creation story mentions the creation of wild animals both before and after the creation of man. Why twice? First, allegorizing ethically ($\dot{\eta}\vartheta\iota\varkappa\tilde{\omega}\varsigma$), this means that wickedness, the beasts, is abundant and is continually being produced. Second, allegorizing naturally ($\varphi\upsilon\sigma\iota\varkappa\tilde{\omega}\varsigma$), the first creation of the animals represents the making of the genera of the passions, and the second creation depicts the making of the species of passions.[10] The same passage of Scripture

---

[9] Although W. Völker, *Fortschritt und Vollendung bei Philo von Alexandrien* (*Texte und Untersuchungen zur Geschichte der altchristlichen Literatur*, Bd. 49), Leipzig, 1939, p. 43, dismisses the suggestion, S. Sandmel, *Philo's Place in Judaism*, Cincinnati, 1956, p. 100, agrees with G. Kuhlmann's conclusion, *Theologia Naturalis bei Philon und bei Paulus* (*Neutestamentliche Forschungen* Heft 7), Gütersloh, 1930, that Philo's unfolding of the individual's experience is a religious existentialism somewhat like the kind of interpretation fashionable because of Kierkegaard.

[10] Cf. the two contrasting allegories side by side, physical and ethical, in *QG* III 3, and *LA* I 39. The term φυσικῶς goes back to earlier Greek allegorists who used it for the hidden meaning of the myths which they took to be des-

renders up two separate allegories which stand side by side, an ethical and a naturalistic one. In the same way, the ladder of Jacob can mean (1) the air inhabited by unbodied souls, (2) the soul in which the divine words move up and down, (3) the life of the ascetic which oscillates back and forth, and (4) the ups and downs of fortune seen in ordinary life (*Som.* I 133–156). Several different interpretations are offered also for the Cherubim who guard Paradise (*Cher.* 21–28), the ark of the covenant with its Cherubim (*Mos.* II 95–100), and the tree of life (*QG* I 10).[11]

These different meanings on the allegorical level can sometimes be disclosed by the different shades of thought in the key words of the text. Gen. 3.16, "And to thy husband shall be thy resort," has two allegorical meanings. Here ἀνήρ can be taken in two senses—as a lawful husband, or as a seducer. Therefore according to one meaning the seducer of sense perception, the woman, is that which sense perception sees and is attracted by. According

---

cribing natural phenomena. In the myths the gods represented natural objects such as sun, moon, and planets, all in their natural movements; Pépin, *op. cit.*, p. 50. Plutarch warns that allegorizing the mythical gods as physical objects may "unintentionally resolve divine powers" into physical phenomena; *De Is.* 377C, R. Hersman, *op. cit.*, p. 52. The word and its cognates became a synonym for "allegorical," and we sometimes find it in Philo in this undifferentiated sense; R. Grant, *op. cit.*, pp. 39–40; *Mut.* 60; *Fug.* 179; *Som.* I 120; *Abr.* 99. Colson in a note at *Abr.* 99 points out that Philo's occasional use of the word almost as an equivalent for "theology" rests upon the Stoic close affinity of divinity and Nature. But Philo sometimes employs "physical" in its original sense to indicate a naturalistic allegory, as in the contrast with the "ethical" sense just seen (*LA* II 5, 6; *QG* III 3; *Abr.* 241). P. Heinisch, *op. cit.*, pp. 10–11, speaking of the distinction between "physical" and "ethical" allegories which goes back to the Greek schools, says: "The physical interpretations relate to the nature of things, and the ethical interpretations seek to develop the moral truths contained in the Homeric narrations." He adds that the gods usually stood for natural forces, and the heroes and heroines for the various virtues. The gods, of course, were allegorized as moral properties too, since they were characterized by certain moral traits which naturally lead to such understandings; Pépin, *op. cit.*, p. 50. "Physical" and "ethical" allegories were not mutually exclusive among Greek writers, just as they were allowed to stand side by side in Philo. R. Hersman, *op. cit.*, p. 11, remarks that Anaxagoras, the first to publish a book on physical allegory, was also the first "to explain the Homeric poems as discussions of virtue and justice."

[11] The manifold layers of meaning in the Biblical texts prompted the rabbis to liken the Word of God to a stone which emits many sparks under the hammer of the expositor; *Sanh.* 34a; b. *Schab.* 88bb; F. Büchsel, TWNT I, p. 203.

to another sense man as the lawful husband is the mind which profits sense perception when it is inwardly directed (*LA* III 220–221). The same principle of the ambiguity of words leading to multiple meanings is the basis for Philo's discourses on "drunkenness," with five different meanings (*Ebr.* 4ff.), and on "fleeing" with three different meanings (*Fug.* 2ff.).

2: The Inspiration of the Prophets

When the scripture says, "About sunset an ecstasy fell upon Abraham" (Gen. 15.15), the LXX term ἔκστασις interests Philo very much (*Her.* 249ff.). "This type of thing is wont to happen to the prophetic kind," he says (*ibid.* 265). Discussing the same passage in *QG* III 9, Philo defines such prophetic ecstasy as "nothing else than the departing and going out of the understanding." The prophet is thus "carried away out of himself" (*Mos.* II 188). Seized by ecstasy his mind is lifted beyond the sense perceptible world to another dimension (*QG* IV 90). This is accomplished by an inspiration of the divine Spirit which comes upon the prophet and "enthuses" him (*Her.* 258, 263). By such descriptions Philo gives the ecstasy of the Biblical prophets a Platonic interpretation. In *Tim.* 71 D and E, and *Phaedrus* 244 D mania or ecstasy is the coming in of the divine Spirit and the exodus of the human spirit. A prophet becomes "possessed" (*Her.* 249; 264; *Mig.* 84), or "carried by God" (*Mos.* II 246; *Her.* 258). Because the prophet is lifted outside himself in ecstasy as the Spirit enters him and displaces his own mind, Philo says, "A prophet . . . has no utterance of his own, but all his utterance came from elsewhere, the echoes of another's voice" (*Her.* 259). He sums up the above ideas in *Spec.* IV 49:

> For a prophet declares nothing at all his own, but is an interpreter of Another who prompts him as he brings forth all his oracles. During the whole time he is enthused, *he is ignorant of what he is saying*—indeed his very rationality is withdrawn, having yielded the castle of the soul, since the divine Spirit has come in to visit and dwell, and plays upon and raises sounds from all the vocal organs for a clear meaning of what the prophet foretells.

In what sense does Philo mean the prophet is ignorant of what he says? We have seen he regards Moses as having been aware of the meanings, literal and allegorical, of what he wrote.[12] Since prophecy includes Scripture writing (*Mos.* II 40; *Prob.* 80), we must conclude that it is inconsistent for Philo to say on the one hand that the prophet writing Scripture intended certain meanings, and on the other hand to declare that he was so rapt in ecstasy that he was ignorant of what he was saying. But the idea of prophetic ignorance is again repeated in *Spec.* I 65 where he says the prophet under divine inspiration "has no power of apprehension when he speaks," serving as channel for God's words prompted to him. Philo pictures the angel inspiring the prophet Balaam speaking thus:

> "I shall prompt the needful words without your mind's consent, and direct your organs of speech as justice and convenience require. I shall guide the reins of speech, and, though you understand it not, employ your tongue for each prophetic utterance." (*Mos.* I 274)

So we must take Philo seriously when he says that while the prophet is under inspiration "he is ignorant of what he is saying." Plato had similarly asserted that the prophet when inspired does not himself understand what he is saying (*Meno* 99 C; *Phaedrus* 245 A, B; *Ion* 533 Df.; *Apol.* 22 BC).[13]

Being in no human form, God did not write his Law by hand. As he created the world through intermediaries, so also he commanded the Law and it was written by others (*QE* II 42). God required a mediator for even those commandments Scripture alleges that he wrote himself. Philo does not apparently regard as prophecies the parts of the Scriptures in which the prophet delivers a direct mandate spoken by God as in the Decalogue. In these cases the prophet is merely a stenographer to the deity, or "interpreter." This, says Philo, is not prophecy in the strict sense of the term, but rather the prophet's representing God, speaking his words to his people as a translator or interpreter (*Mos.* II 188–191). What Philo understands as prophecies are not verbal oracles given by God through the prophet, but the words of the prophet himself, τὰ ἰδιαίτερα, while he is under divine inspiration (*ibid.* 188).[14]

---

[12] See above, p. 26.

[13] On this point see J. Tate, "Plato and Allegorical Interpretation," *CQ* 1929, p. 148, and "On the History of Allegorism," *CQ*, 1934, p. 113.

[14] H. Wolfson, *op. cit.*, II, p. 41 f., thinks that in this distinction between prophecy and interpretation we find a reference to the difference between the receiver of visions and the one who interpreted them, a refinement in Plato and in classical Greek writers. When Philo says "interpretation and

Therefore he distinguishes between the general laws spoken by God which are contained in the Decalogue, and the particular laws which the prophet Moses spoke while filled with the divine Spirit and which are prophecies in the true sense (*Dec.* 175). The latter laws, however, are none the less regarded as oracles (*Mos.* II 67, 69).

Wolfson has studied what amount to the four main functions of prophecy in Philo, showing their partial derivation from the Bible, and their agreement with the four kinds of inspiration called "frenzy," or "mania," in Plato.[15] First, the prophet standing under mantic inspiration possesses the power to foretell the future. Philo gives two examples of this predictive prophetic power in commenting on Abraham's ecstatic experience. Noah was a prophet. Under divine possession he was able to see the future and so cursed and blessed future generations. Jacob foresaw the future and proclaimed it to his children (*Her.* 260–261).[16]

---

prophecy are not the same thing," he contrasts prophecy as the receiving of oracles with the interpretation of them. When he says elsewhere, "prophets are interpreters of God" (*Spec.* III 7, IV 49), he is reminding his Greek readers, familiar with the distinction between prophecy and interpretation, that in the Bible no such distinction exists. The prophet is interpreter of his own oracles, although, as he points out in this passage, there is a distinction between the two in Greek. Wolfson's suggestion is a valuable help in understanding what Philo apparently means when he says, "prophets are interpreters of God." He means, in point of fact, all prophets in the Bible happen to be interpreters of God, although the two functions themselves are not the same. But the distinction between the functions of prophecy and interpretation in *Mos.* II 188 Wolfson misunderstands. For Philo's distinction here is not as Wolfson thinks between one who receives and one who interprets oracles, although the terms "interpretation" or "interpreter" used for the explaining or expositor of oracles can be found very often in other passages (cf. *Dec.* 175). Philo is distinguishing between "the things more especially his" (Moses'), τὰ ἰδιαίτερα, and the divine utterances spoken by God through the prophet as interpreter. The fact that Philo elsewhere contradicts himself and speaks of the Decalogue as having been miraculously spoken by God alone (*Dec.* 19), by means of a voice produced in the air (*Dec.* 33), does not concern us here. Thus, that which is to be interpreted is not the oracle already given by God, but God himself, So prophecy is something spoken by the prophet, albeit under divine inspiration. Inspiration, in this sense, means the prophet's acting as medium for words spoken by God. But the same prophet is involved in both cases.

[15] *Ibid.*, pp. 11–22.

[16] Cf. also *Som.* I 1; II 2,3; E. Herriot, *Philon le Juif*, Paris, 1898, p. 196. Bréhier, *op. cit.*, p. 186, concludes that for Philo there is no essential differ-

Another function of the prophetic *mania* is the legislation of laws. In discussing the ecstasy of Abraham in Gen. 15.12, Philo describes it as a knowledge by which oracles and laws are legislated by God (*QG* III 9). Now in fact the only Biblical prophet who appears in the Pentateuch in the law-giving capacity is Moses, and in his treatise *On the Life of Moses II* Philo portrays Moses as king, law-giver, high priest, and prophet (292 *et passim*). However the word "prophet" used here by Philo is not a separate term alongside the others, but rather is a general one including them. For as Philo turns in this tract to the prophetic office of Moses, having discussed the other three immediately before, he enumerates three prophetic activities, two of which have to do with law-giving. By acting as "interpreter" (in the sense we defined above) for God, the prophet mediates God-given legislation and becomes a law-giver. In putting questions to God while under prophetic inspiration, the prophet receives divine instruction and again is a mediator of legislation (*Mos.* II 188–190). Hence law-giving is an aspect of prophecy. Elsewhere Moses is introduced as "the chief of the

---

ence between the prophetic oracles received while awake or in dreams; see *Jos.* 95. His idea of revelation of the future in dreams agrees with that of Stoics such as Posidonius; cf. Cicero, *De Divin.* I 63; H. Leisegang, *Der Heilige Geist* I/I, Leipzig, 1919, p. 180. However the general notion seems to have been common among all peoples in antiquity. The Stoics Antipater and Posidonius took up the legend that Socrates under the influence of his daimonion often had predicted future events; M. Pohlenz, *Die Stoa* I, Göttingen, 1948, pp. 186; 231. The Stoics taught that the possibility of mantic prediction of future events lay in the natural mutual sympathy of all parts in the universe's structure, preordained by Providence. Everything in the future is predetermined and has its seed in the present. Therefore men as members of the organism of the world are sensitive to changes elsewhere in the causal nexus, and by mantic experience receive premonitions of the future; *ibid.*, pp. 198, 217, 232. In *Mig.* 180 Philo states Moses accepts the Stoic doctrine of the interdependence of all parts of the universe and their sympathetic affinity, but rejects their theology. But I have not been able to find any evidence that Philo laid mantic prediction to the organism of all things, or even to Providence.

The Stoics also likened mantic inspiration to death, because in both there occurs the separation of the soul from the body. The bodiless soul in mantic ecstasy is then free for communion with the divine Spirit, and so the possibility of clairvoyance; *ibid.*, p. 232f. The Egyptian Stoic Chaeremon witnesses that after death the Egyptian believer, being separated from the body, receives mantic power and a clairvoyant understanding; H. R. Schwyzer, *Chairemon, Klassisch-philologische Studien* 4, Leipzig, 1932, fr. 9.

prophets," and because he is in touch with divine things and speaks in oracles, he has "the power of language to express prophet-like the holy laws" (*Mut.* 125–126).[17]

The priestly function for Philo is also under the heading of prophecy. Philo states "the true priest is necessarily a prophet" (*Spec.* IV 192), and says that Moses "armed with prophetic knowledge" is able to worship God as high priest (*Praem.* 56). In the latter passage he adds that one function of this prophetic priest is to offer thanksgiving for the people when they do good, and to make supplications for propitiation when they go astray.

Thus the prophet sums up in himself the roles of visionary, law-giver, and propitiator. These three functions correspond to the first three types of inspiration or frenzy given by Plato in *Phaedrus* 244 D ff. There Plato explains that the first type of frenzy is that of divination by which the one inspired foretells future events. The second type is the frenzy of the priest by which through rites, prayers, purifications, or worship the oracular power rescues men from such things as disease. Third is the frenzy of the Muses which is the inspired source of the laws of legislators and kings.[18] The fourth type of inspiration is the frenzy of the philosopher through which he recalls intelligible ideas which lie beyond the sensible world.

Philo interestingly also adds this fourth Platonic type of frenzy to his understanding of prophecy. He asserts that prophets and priests have refused citizenship in the sensible world, and have been translated into the commonwealth of imperishable and incorporeal ideas (*Gig.* 61). There the prophet is given the full and clear apprehension of things perceivable to the understanding but invisible to the senses (*Spec.* IV 192).[19]

---

[17] In *Cong.* 132 law-giving and prophecy are mentioned together as gifts given in divine inspiration.

[18] See also *Meno* 99 D.

[19] Plato had insisted that the dialectic method is still necessary to get at truth, and that inspiration is no substitute for it. Indeed he even scorned any short-cutting of dialectic in arriving at truth; *Phaedrus* 277, J. Tate, "On the History of Allegorism," *CQ*, 1934, p. 14. But in Philo Bezalel who learns by dialectic is in an inferior position to Moses who learns by a direct vision of the heavenly archetypes (*LA* III 100–103; *Plant.* 26–27). Here Plato rather than Philo represents the general Greek intellectual restraint toward intuitive "mantic" inspiration. Nothing was more ridiculed by Greek comedies than this type of inspiration; H. Leisegang, *Der Heilige Geist*, p. 131 f.

It is in such a state of divine possession ($\varkappa\alpha\tau o\varkappa\omega\chi\dot{\eta}$) that the prophets composed the Scriptures (*Prob.* 80), which are infallible in every way (*Abr.* 258). Philo writes similarly about the translators of the LXX. These men were not actual translators, but prophets. They became "enthused" with divine inspiration and thus "prophesied." Each scribe's translation agreed with that of his neighbor, as though all had received the translation from an invisible prompter (*Mos.* II 37, 40). He calls them "hierophants," i.e., priests of secret mysteries, a term he uses elsewhere to describe Moses (*LA* III 23, 173; *Sac.* 94, *Post.* 16) and the prophet Jeremiah's holy function.[20] The result of this inspired prophetic work was an infallible translation of the Hebrew text, differing in no detail from the original and corresponding literally with it— a marvel to any reader who knows both languages and who ever compares the miraculous agreement of the two texts (*Mos.* II 37 to 40).[21]

Philo, then, took over the Greek and particularly the Platonic theory of mantic inspiration. His Jewish faith in an inerrant Biblical text was confirmed when he imputed this inspiration to its prophetic

---

[20] *Cher.* 49. At this passage he borrows a terminology from the Eleusinian mysteries by representing Moses as the "greater" and the prophets as the "lesser" mysteries; cf. also *Sac.* 62 and Colson and Whitaker's note. In *Her.* 69 Philo uses the words $\beta\alpha\chi\chi\varepsilon\dot{u}\omega$ and $\varkappa o\rho u\beta\iota\dot{\alpha}\omega$, two terms from the Greek mysteries which referred to inspired frenzy in the Bacchic and Corybantic mysteries, and applies them to prophetic possession.

[21] From such a description it ought to be quite clear that Philo never compared, nor was able to compare, the Hebrew text with his LXX copy. Indeed to a writer who held such a view of the LXX the Hebrew Bible and ability to read it would have been superfluous, since he presupposed that the Greek was as authoritative as the original. Wolfson, *op. cit.* I, p. 90, offers no evidence for saying that Philo checked the Hebrew against the Greek whenever necessary. Frequently Philo bases exegetical points on actual mistaken LXX translations; C. Siegfried, *op. cit.*, p. 142. H. Ryle's efforts, *Philo and the Holy Scripture*, London, 1895, to show Philo's numerous textual readings that often agree with the Masoretic text rather than the LXX prove only that Philo's Greek copy frequently diverges from those that have come down to us, at the same time coinciding with the Hebrew. For a few examples of Philo's many erroneous etymologies of Hebrew names, see E. Stein, *Die allegorische Exegese des Philo aus Alexandreia*, pp. 21–26. Before he published the English translations, R. Marcus in a private letter informed S. Sandmel, *op. cit.*, p. 13 n. 21, that he had found unmistakable evidence that Philo knew Hebrew in sections of *QE* and *QG*. What this evidence is, Marcus does not tell us in his edition.

authors, for by such frenzy the visionaries' minds were displaced by the divine Spirit and permitted superhuman insights.

3: Prophecy as a Mystical Interpretation of Scripture

Philo sees the scripture, then, (1) as given by prophets while under the hypnotic spell of the divine Spirit, often writing of things they themselves did not understand, and (2) as containing multiple meanings, the most important of which lie buried on the hidden level accessible only by allegorical interpretation. If the decisive meaning of scripture was partially obscure to its writers and remains concealed by its literal clothing, how does the exegete go about uncovering it?

Philo would have emphatically denied that finding the hidden sense of scripture is purely a matter of ingenuity. Instead he would have insisted that the disclosure of this meaning is given to the exegete as grace from God:

> On some occasions, after making up my mind to follow the usual course of writing on philosophical tenets,[22] and knowing definitely the substance of what I was to set down, I have found my understanding incapable of giving birth to a single idea, and have given it up without accomplishing anything, reviling my understanding for its self-conceit, and filled with amazement at the might of Him that IS to Whom is due the opening and closing of the soulwombs. On other occasions, I have approached my work empty and suddenly become full, the ideas falling in a shower from above and being sown invisibly, so that under the influence of the Divine possession I have been filled with corybantic frenzy and have been unconscious of anything, place, persons present, myself, words spoken, lines written. For I obtained language, ideas, an enjoyment of light, keenest vision, pellucid distinctness of objects, such as might be received through the eyes as the result of clearest shewing. (*Mig.* 34–35).

The phrase "under the influence of the Divine possession I have been filled with corybantic frenzy . . ." ($\dot{\upsilon}\pi\dot{o}$ $\varkappa\alpha\tau o\chi\tilde{\eta}\varsigma$ $\dot{\varepsilon}\nu\vartheta\acute{\varepsilon}o\upsilon$ $\varkappa o\varrho\upsilon\beta\alpha\nu\tau\iota\tilde{\alpha}\nu$) interests us especially. The words $\varkappa\alpha\tau o\chi\tilde{\eta}\varsigma$ $\dot{\varepsilon}\nu\vartheta\acute{\varepsilon}o\upsilon$ are applied in the synonymous form $\dot{\varepsilon}.$ $\varkappa\alpha\tau o\varkappa\omega\chi\dot{\eta}$[23] to the mantic inspiration of the prophets in *Mig.* 84; *Her.* 249; *Prob.* 80, and in *Her.* 264 in connection with mantic inspiration in general. Philo uses $\varkappa o\varrho.$ in the

---

[22] Philo refers to expositing scripture as philosophy in *Som.* I 127.

[23] For a statement of the significance of $\varkappa\alpha\tau o\chi\dot{\eta}$ as divine ecstatic possession in the mystery cults, see R. Reitzenstein, *Die hellenistischen Mysterienreligionen,*[3] Leipzig, 1927, pp. 197–211.

participle form as a description of the mantic power which inspires one enabling him to foretell the future, a fundamental prophetic ability for him. Hence in *Mig.* 34f. he claims for himself the same prophetic inspiration as he comments on scripture, i.e., "writing on philosophical tenets," as the prophets who wrote the Bible were given.

We have seen that Philo thought of the prophets as having been given superhuman knowledge, saying things they often did not understand. In the same way he states in the above passage, "I have been ... unconscious of anything ... myself, words spoken, lines written." Elsewhere he says that a Word often comes to his soul allowing it to divine through mantic inspiration things which it does not itself know. Through such an inspiration he received the allegorical interpretation of the Cherubim in Gen. 3.24. They are symbols of the powers or attributes of God, his sovereignty and goodness (*Cher.* 27, 28). Once more the "familiar invisible spirit" instructed Philo as to the Spiritual meaning of the name "Jerusalem." According to this inspiration, Jerusalem translated means "vision of peace." Therefore anyone who crosses over to God the true Peace may "justly be called the dwelling-place and city of God" (*Som.* II 250–254). This interpretation, he says, was "prompted" him (ὑπηχεῖ) by the Spirit. In *Som.* I 164 he urges that the lessons gained from a study of the symbolic meanings of the different names of God ought to be enough to move the blind literalists beyond the letter to seek the real meaning of the sacred oracles. Therefore he prays to God, the Great Hierophant, using the same verb as above, that he may "prompt" us,[24] "conducting us as a mystagogue to the hidden light of the hallowed words," that he may show us secrets of the Scriptures, "the fast-locked lovelinesses invisible to the uninitiate." Again the verb appears in *Som.* II 2 used to describe God's "prompting" of revelations in dreams, unclear to us, but known to him. The interpretation offered in this study that the inspiration of the Biblical writer and the allegorical interpreter are of the same prophetic type is further strengthened in *Mut.* 139 where Philo uses the same verb which he applies to God's "prompting" the prophet Hosea to speak an oracle.

---

[24] On this special meaning of the verb in Philo, see Colson and Whitaker's note at *Som.* I 164.

We understand, then, that for Philo prophecy is both the giving of the revelation to the writers of the Scripture and the uncovering of its hidden meaning by the later interpreter.[25] Both writer and interpreter are seized by divine possession, in one case writing, in another interpreting.[26] The giving and the finding again of the revelation, now disclosed by allegorical exegesis, is like a great mystery. Therefore Philo borrows words and thought forms from the mystery cults to express the secret truths given the Biblical writers and the mystery disclosed by the interpreter of Scripture.[27]

The divine Spirit leading like a hierophant opens up the hidden meanings of Scripture to Philo as to a prophet in a mystery religion. But the allegorical truths remain obscure to all other Biblical

---

[25] After concluding that Philo actually believed that God had descended upon him as he did upon the prophets of old, M. Pohlenz, *Philon von Alexandreia* (*Nachrichten von der Akademie der Wissenschaften in Göttingen, phil.-hist.* Kl., 1942, Nr. 5), p. 473f., goes on to point out that Philo never refers to himself as having had an *ecstatic* experience. If Philo does not happen to use the word "ecstasy" to characterize his own experience, this silence is not enough to distinguish Philo's commentator's prophetic inspiration from the Biblical writers'. W. Völker, *op. cit.*, p. 314, even states that Philo's using sometimes one and sometimes another ecstatic phraseology shows an obvious vacillation in his thinking and is a clear proof that he never experienced an ecstatic state himself. But an opposite conclusion could be drawn reasoning that Philo is instead setting forth the magnificent variety of ecstatic rapture from personal experience.

[26] Another indication that Alexandrian Judaism believed that prophecy continued through all generation is *Wisd.* 7.27 in which it is said that Wisdom in every generation "passes into holy souls and makes them friends of God, and prophets."

[27] R. Grant, *op. cit.*, p. 131f., calls attention to the general association of terms from the mystery religions, such as we find in the passages here considered, with the allegorical method. Heraclitus calls Homer "the great hierophant of heaven and the gods;" H. Arnim, *op. cit.* II, 100.9; cf. 85.8. He mentions initiation into the mystic wisdom of the Homeric rites (75.18). Also the allegorical method leads to the "divine rites of Homer" (85.8). He evidently refers to Homer's poems allegorically interpreted as "the mystic discourses of the theology of the ineffable rites" (10.8). Clement of Alexandria used similar language with respect to allegory.

Philo, of course, uses language and ideas taken from the mystery religions throughout his writings, and not just in reference to allegorical truths; cf. *Fug.* 85; *LA* III 100. For a discussion of other such motifs of the mysteries in Alexandrian Jewish literature, such as the LXX translation of Proverbs, and the *Wisdom of Solomon*, see H. Lewy, *Sobria Ebrietas* (ZNW Beih. 9), Giessen, 1929, pp. 15–17, n. 3, with references to other works on the subject.

readers without this mystic all-illuminating inspiration. He admits that the allegorical sense is obscure to the "many," and is clear only to the "few" who are able to behold the subjective or noetic meanings lying beyond the objective words of the text (*Abr.* 200, 147, 236). These "horatic men" (*Plant.* 36) are of course to be identified with the school of allegorical exegetes in Alexandria which Philo represents.[28] As we might have anticipated, Philo frequently refers to his school of fellow-allegorists in the same mystic language which he has used to describe his own illuminating experiences. He addresses them in the formula, "O initiates, whose ears are purified!" (*Cher.* 48; *Gig.* 54)[29] as opposed to those who are "uninitiated" in "allegory and the nature-truth which loves to conceal its meaning" (*Fug.* 179). Since Scripture's allegorical message can never be grasped by those who do not share in the mystical illumination which makes it known, Philo continues the language of the mysteries in admonishing his colleagues not to try to impart their esoteric knowledge of the mysteries to the literalists[30] because the latter lack the essential gift to understand it anyway (*Cher.* 42, 48; *Sac.* 60, 62).

---

[28] See above, p. 18f.

[29] Heraclitus also refers to allegorists as purified for their work; see Grant, *op. cit.*, p. 9.

[30] Colson and Whitaker have translated δεισιδαίμονες and related words in *Cher.* 42; *Immut.* 163; *Praem.* 40 and elsewhere as "the superstitious" or those "who corrupt religion into superstition." It was a term of reproach used by philosophers such as Hecataeus of Abdera, and Posidonius against the rites and cults of Judaism and other religions. But I. Heinemann, *Philons griechische und jüdische Bildung*, Breslau, 1932, p. 453f., declares that it was only very tenuously connected with superstition, that it rather referred to "extreme anxiety and zeal in observing religious ordinances." Diognetus (I; IV 1) mentions Judaism as "the δεισιδαιμονία of the Jews," and applies the term to Sabbath observance. But the word also could be used in the favorable sense of "God-fearing;" H. Bolkestein, *Theophrastos Charakter der Deisidaimonia als religionsgeschichtliche Urkunde* (RVV 21, Heft 2), Giessen, 1929, pp. 8–10. Philo, however, picks up a word of contempt used against Judaism by its opponents and applies it to the literalists who could not or refused to study the scripture allegorically. Plutarch similarly called the literal understanding of the myths δεισιδαιμονία; *De Is.* 355 D, *et passim.*

CHAPTER III

Interpretation of the Law

1: The Law beyond the Torah

When Philo states that the patriarchs were "living and vocal laws" (ἔμψυχοι καὶ λογικοὶ νόμοι, *Abr.* 5; *Mos.* I 162; II 4), or "unwritten laws" (*Dec.* 1; *Abr.* 276), he is saying that they led a virtuous life (*Virt.* 194) even before the revelation of the written Torah, living by the unwritten Law (*ibid.*; *Abr.* 61). It was a Midrashic teaching that the patriarchs followed the Torah before it had been given.[1] But that the unwritten Law which they followed according to Philo corresponds to nothing in normative Judaism, such as the oral tradition of the scribes,[2] or the Torah which was created before the world,[3] is shown by Philo's conclusion that Abraham did the divine Law and commandments "not taught by written words, but unwritten nature gave him the zeal to follow where wholesome and untainted impulse led him" (*Abr.* 275). Thus Philo is saying the Law is harmonized with unwritten Nature.

The attempt to unite Law and Nature was made by Plato in his proposed legislation for the republic (*Rep.* V 456C). In the philosophical tradition following there came the feeling that the written laws of the state were actually inferior to the unwritten Law, whether the latter be custom or the Law of Nature.[4] An effort by legislators to harmonize the written laws of the state with the unwritten Law of Nature was therefore urged. For laws

---

[1] *Midr. Tanch.* to Gen. 15.1, ed. Buber p. 71; E. Stein, *Philo und der Midrash*, BZAW 57, 1931, p. 26; *Kidd.* IV 14; S. Rosenblatt, *The Interpretation of the Bible in the Mishnah*, Baltimore, 1935, p. 3.

[2] I. Heinemann, "Die Lehre vom ungeschriebenen Gesetz im jüdischen Schrifttum," HUCA, 1927, pp. 147 ff.

[3] *Gen. R.* I, 4; E. Stein, *Philo und der Midrash*, p. 3.

[4] R. Hirzel, ΑΓΡΑΦΟΣ ΝΟΜΟΣ (*Abhandlungen der sächsischen Gesellschaft, philol.-hist. Klasse* xx), Leipzig, 1900, pp. 1–20.

to be true laws should mirror Nature since "the true laws are images of the cosmic laws," as Proclus said.[5]

But then certain Hellenistic thinkers tried to find a universal and eternal Law within men's souls as well as in the cosmos.[6] Such a Law would be higher than the conventional and various written laws of states. To quote Proclus again:

> The true laws have no need of being written in letters, but rather are laid down and remain immovable in the souls of those who live by them. Customs are matters of both private and public concern among all persons; but certain people are living laws, and follow laws of a different kind than the physiological ones governing the animals, or the political laws under which men are subject.[7]

Living according to this inward *nomos emsychos*, the ruler would not need the written laws to guide him. Plutarch says this inward Law would be the Logos within man:

> Who, then shall rule the ruler? The
>
> > Law, the king of all
> > both mortals and immortals,
>
> as Pindar says—not law written outside him in books or on wooden tablets or the like, but reason endowed with life (λόγος ἔμψυχος) within him, always abiding with him and watching over him and never leaving his soul without its leadership.[8]

By stating that Abraham, Isaac, and Jacob, prior to the giving of the written Law, had in their souls the Law on which the written Law is based, Philo means to give the Torah a certain support and justification which Hellenism's criticism of the written laws of communities and states at the time demanded. Philo was saying, if philosophy minimizes written law in its search for a higher Law of Nature, or one written on men's souls, let that be no pretext for overlooking Moses' written Law. For it is a memorial to such an inward Law, having first been engraved on the patriarchs' souls. Therefore he says that the enacted laws of the Torah "are nothing else than memorials of the life of the

---

[5] *Procli Diadochi in Platonis rem publicam commentarii* II, ed. W. Kroll, Leipzig, 1901, p. 307 1. 15.

[6] H. Kleinknecht, TWNT IV, p. 1027.

[7] Op. cit., p. 307, 11. 7–13.

[8] *Ad principem ineruditem 780 C*, tr. H. R. Fowler, Loeb Classical Library, London, 1936.

ancients, preserving to a later generation their actual words and deeds" (*Abr.* 5). The Law of Nature itself was engraved on the souls of the patriarchs, and it is also the basis of the O.T. legislation, since the latter is a written copy of the words and deeds of the "living and vocal laws," the patriarchs, who lived according to Nature (*Mig.* 127f.). Because the Law of Nature is also "unwritten Law," the patriarchs in harmony with Nature's Law are also "unwritten laws" (*Dec.* 1; *Abr.* 276).

It is Philo's thesis that the laws of Moses answer the requirements of genuine law, being "the most similar image" or likeness (ἐικών) "of the cosmic law (πολιτεία[9])" (*Mos.* II 51). He refers to Moses' laws as "stamped with the seals of nature" (*Mos.* II 14). He goes on:

> Thus whoever will carefully examine the nature of the particular enactments will find that they seek to attain to the harmony of the universe and are in agreement with the principles of eternal nature (*Mos.* II 52).

Elsewhere he refers to these principles of eternal nature as "the Law of Nature," or Orthos Logos,[10] according to which God governs his universe (*Spec.* III 189; *QE* II 42; *Opif.* 143; *Prob.* 47; *Jos.* 31), just as the Greek *polis* was governed according to constitutional law.[11] Thus in giving Israel's Torah, God at the same time prescribed it as a Law for the world "for the chosen race is a likeness of the world, and its Law (is a likeness of the laws) of the world" (*QE* II 42).

In declaring that the Torah is a likeness[12] of the cosmic law, Philo gave Judaism's faith in the eternity of the Torah[13] a firm philosophical basis. If the laws are as indelible as Nature which

---

[9] For πολιτεία as a synonym for "law," see *Conf.* 2; *Jos.* 29.

[10] Synonyms in Stoicism and Philo; see Colson and Whitaker's note at *Ebr.* 142; M. Pohlenz, *Die Stoa* I, p. 61; II, p. 35.

[11] The universal Law of Nature like the Logos for the Stiocs was not only the principle of structure and order in the world, but also the governing principle to which men and gods were subject; see *ibid.* I, p. 132. Philo's concept of the Law of Nature is modified somewhat from the Stoic view. It has nothing to do with εἱμαρμένη and ἀνάγκη, for Nature operates according to specific laws and ordinances laid down by God who is ultimately free and not bound by conditions of Nature (*Her.* 300f.; *QG* I 21; *Plant.* 8f.; *Opif.* 61; *Agr.* 51.

[12] Not identity, as F. Geiger, *Philon von Alexandreia als sozialer Denker* (*Tübinger Beiträge zur Altertumswissenschaft*, XIV), Stuttgart, 1932.

[13] See below p. 113 n. 26.

they faithfully portray, then we can confidently assert that they will endure as long as the sun, moon, and universe—in fact as long as Nature itself (*Mos.* II 14; *Ebr.* 142). Philo also thereby exempted Moses' laws from the relativizing critique of the Stoics which denied absolute value to any people's laws, since the conflicting laws of different nations cancel each other out, and indeed amount to human superficialities which obscure and obstruct Nature's Law (*Jos.* 28–31). Philo repeats this critique himself:.

> What is base with us is noble with others . . . our lawful their unlawful . . . (*Ebr.* 193–194). We may fairly say that mankind from east to west, every country and nation and state, shew aversion to foreign institutions, and think that they will enhance the respect for their own by shewing disrespect for those of other countries (*Mos.* II 19).

If the Stoics sought a metaphysical Law which would be binding on all men at all times,[14] that metaphysical Law could be found stamped in the Torah.

Philo realized he could hardly expect Gentiles to accept Moses' laws simply on the claim that they were of divine origin—an assertion made for the Cretan and Lacedaemonian laws as well to name only two.[15] For Philo's apology for the Jewish laws it makes no difference whether Moses was an interpreter of divine laws as oracles (which Philo certainly believed he was), or simply a legislator for the Jewish nation (*Mos.* I 1). To gain a hearing he had to show that the Jewish laws were likenesses of a higher Law which the Hellenistic world recognized as the only basis for valid legislation. The Stoics had asserted that virtue is attained when one brings his life into harmony with Nature.[16] In his treatise *On the Virtues* Philo argues that the Biblical laws, laid down in accord with the Law of Nature, can indeed be summed up under the headings of four main virtues: courage, humanity, repentance, and nobility (*Virt.* 15–17; 127). In his treatises *On the Decalogue* and *On the Special Laws I–IV* he exposits first the Ten Commandments, then many of the other O.T. laws with the apologetic purpose of showing the harmony between them and Nature, or the Law of Nature. A few examples will here suffice.

---

[14] M. Pohlenz, *Die Stoa* I, pp. 132 ff.; see also Colson's notes at *Jos.* 28 and 29.

[15] Plato, *Laws* I, 624 A–B; *Minos* 320 B; H. Wolfson, *Philo* II, p. 15.

[16] M. Pohlenz, *Die Stoa* I, pp. 119–123.

The Decalogue itself rhymes with Nature's perfect number, ten, according to Pythagorean number philosophy (*Dec.* 20–31). The commandment to honor one's parents is validated by observing the same principle among the animals who live "by Nature (*Dec.* 106–117). Murder, proscribed in the sixth commandment, disrupts the social harmony inherent in mankind and therefore subverts the laws of Nature (*Dec.* 132). The commandment against stealing is issued because theft can become a habit stronger than Nature which would have us respect others' property and in time the practice can grow to threaten the whole community (*Dec.* 135 to 137). Covetousness, forbidden by the last commandment, if left unchecked will finally result in all life's matters being directed against Nature (*Dec.* 150). The laws against pederasty justly oppose anyone who "debases the morals of Nature" (*Spec.* III 38). The extension of the Sabbath rest to slaves is because no man is a slave by Nature (*Spec.* II 69).[17] Interdicting the cross-breeding of animals follows the harmony of the Law of Nature (*Spec.* IV 203f.). The legislation in Deut. 25.11f. enforcing modesty is in strict keeping with the statutes of Nature (*Spec.* III 175–177). The Law forbids planting two kinds of fruit on the same ground, for such is "excessive avarice, and this is a vice which upsets the laws of nature," ruining the productivity of the ground and plants (*Spec.* IV 203–212). Without going further into Philo's understanding of the Law of Nature we may point out in passing how dominant the thought of "harmony" as opposed to chaos is in these few examples. The Law of Nature brings all the parts and members of man, the state, and the cosmos into their natural harmonious relationship one to another according to the classic Greek definition of righteousness.

Philo's effort to show that the Law is "ever desirous to follow the course of nature" (*Spec.* II 129; *Virt.* 18f.) may have helped to make the laws of Moses more plausible to some, but the same apology served also to weaken the authority of the Torah. When he declared that the Torah is a likeness or copy of the Law of Nature, at the same time he set a higher Law *beyond* the Torah, a Law which the Torah at best reflects or agrees with. Philo himself said "every εἰκών by its deceptive resemblance falsifies the original"

---

[17] I. Heinemann, *Philons griechische und jüdische Bildung*, pp. 330ff., and Colson, *ad loc*, give Cynic-Stoic parallels to this non-Jewish idea.

(*Praem.* 29). By making the Torah a likeness of the Law of Nature Philo thereby robbed it of any authority of its own.[18] The patriarchs did not even need the written Torah; and by conforming to the Law of Nature "their whole life was one of happy obedience to law" (*Abr.* 5, 6; cf. 16).[19]

2: The Spiritualization of the Law

A persistent problem for Philo was that the Law often legislated over seemingly insignificant and arbitrary things, and over matters which were on the surface totally unrelated to his philosophical notion of the Law of Nature upon which the Torah was supposedly based. So it was often necessary for him to struggle to find some spiritual meaning contained within or hinted at by certain puzzling or problematic laws. Moses, he says, wishes to train his people in frugality and against the sin of covetousness. Therefore he forbids the enjoyment of tasty pork[20] and scaleless aquatic species (*Spec.* IV 101). For the same reason he forbids the fat (Lev. 3.17) as the richest part of a sacrificial victim to be eaten (*Spec.* IV 124). His reason for forbidding the eating of carnivorous animals was that some are man-eaters, and eating animals which prey on us instills a feeling of revenge in us, which consequently makes us beast-like (*Spec.* IV 103f.). The laws that persons who touch the corpse of one who has died a natural death, or that those having

---

[18] I. Heinemann, "Die Lehre vom ungeschriebenen Gesetz," HUCA, 1927, p. 156, says the reason for this lies" ... in that Greek doctrine that the particular laws of the individual peoples, in comparison with the primal universal Law, may claim no absolute importance, such as was ascribed to the Torah."

[19] Cf. *Abr.* 61 where Philo states that anyone who contemplates the order of Nature has no need of a teacher "to practice a law-abiding and peaceful life," and *Abr.* 11 where the "undying book of nature" is implicitly placed above the written Torah which is merely "pieces of paper which moths shall destroy," in the same way that the Orthos Logos in *Prob.* 46 is not engraved in parchment or slabs but "by immortal nature on the immortal mind."

[20] Plutarch, *De Is.* 354, rejecting the mythical basis for the Egyptians' eating pork at the annual sacrifice to Typho, finds the real reason in the rejection of everything promoting luxury and voluptuousness. Unlike Philo, Plutarch regards pork as a common fare, although both in the same way rationalize religious dietary practices in an effort to point out a profounder truth lying behind them.

had martial intercourse are impure until after proper purification rites (Numb. 19.11ff; Lev. 15.18), far from being pointless ritual, carry great moral value. For as people observe these prescriptions concerning death and sex in circumstances wherein no crime has been committed, they are thereby admonished to shun automatically such crimes as murder and adultery (*Spec.* III 63, 205). The legislation against cross-breeding of animals is to admonish men against unlawful intercourse (*Spec.* III 46).[21]

In these instances Philo seeks to show valid bases for dietary and cleanliness legislation by rather far-fetched speculation on the value thereof for moral education by introducing a symbolic interpretation but without actually losing sight of the literal sense. But certain of the dietary laws proscribing, for instance, the eating of reptiles (Lev. 11.42) Philo justifies on the basis of the symbolism which they spiritually teach. By reptiles Moses means those persons who devote themselves to the belly, upon which reptiles creep. The Law teaches symbolically that such are unclean (*Spec.* IV 113; *LA* III 139; *Mig.* 64f.). On the other hand, the permission to eat the "flying reptiles" (Lev. 11.21) is a symbolic approval to those souls which though rooted to the earthly body nevertheless have strength to soar upward, "exchanging earth for heaven, and corruption for immortality" (*Her.* 239; cf. *LA* II 105). In the same way when Lev. 11.9ff. and Deut. 14.9f. proscribe eating aquatic creatures without fins and scales, again certain persons are really being repudiated. They are those pleasure-loving souls who are carried along by the current, unable to swim against the stream (*Spec.* IV 110–112). The permission to eat animals with cloven hooves and who chew the cud (Lev. 11.3f.; Deut. 14.6f.) contains symbolic admonition. Cud-chewing refers to the process by which we remember the impressions we have been taught, thereby making their apprehension firmly fixed in the mind. But

---

[21] The hermeneutical principle *a minori ad maiore* is involved in the above legislation. In III 48, 117, and IV 104 Philo refers to it as "forbidding from afar" (πόρρωθεν and μακρόθεν). See below pp. 127ff. for a further discussion of this principle. The *Letter of Aristeas* 149 argues that the birds of prey are forbidden as unclean as a symbolic reminder to men to take nothing by violence, reasoning according to the same principle: "For where it is not fitting to touch any of the above-mentioned creatures because of their respective make-ups, how must we in every way take precaution lest our own characters degenerate into this state?"

apprehension alone is useless without the discrimination between the virtuous and evil ways of life symbolized by the parted hoof that we may choose the good and avoid evil (*Spec.* IV 106–108; *Agr.* 145).[22] Discussing the same laws elsewhere Philo admits there is no real rational justification for why the camel which chews the cud but does not part the hoof would be unclean unless the above dietary proscriptions are symbolized (*Agr.* 131).

The ceremonial laws of Judaism also posed a problem for Philo's apology for the Torah. He recalls that the rite of circumcision "is an object of ridicule among many people" (*Spec.* I 1). After mentioning four hygenic reasons for the practice which were passed onto him by others (*Spec.* I 4–8), Philo adds that circumcision also contains two symbolic teachings. It represents the cutting away of pleasures bewitching the mind and the excision of the vain "glory" or "evil opinion" which ascribes to man the creative power which belongs to God alone (*Spec.* I 8–11; *QG* III 48; *Mig.* 92). Throughout his writings Philo tries to demonstrate that the themes of the Jewish festivals contain within them allegorical truths for the soul. So the Day of Atonement is a humiliation of the soul and a putting away of boasting (*Post.* 48). The Passover expresses the soul's crossing from passion and all that is sensible to the noetic and divine (*Cong.* 106; *Sac.* 63; *Spec.* II 147). The leaven used in the loaves during the Feast of Weeks or Pentecost is an outward expression of the inward joy of the soul, for "joy is the rational elevation or rising of the soul" (*Spec.* II 185).[23] The New Moon Feast takes place as the moon receives again its brightness while the sun begins to illuminate it, and this is a moral lesson from the natural bodies instructing man to give freely to the deserving just as the sun gives its light to the moon (*Spec.* II 141). Because the feast takes place at the time when the moon reaches the starting-point at which it began, the feast also teaches us to make our ends to correspond with our beginnings (*Spec.* II 142).

---

[22] That Philo is dependent upon *Aristeas* 150–162 here seems to me beyond question. Not only do both authors say the parted hoof relates to discrimination (διαστολή, *Aristeas* 151, 155, 161; *Spec.* IV 108) and chewing the cud to memory (μνήμη, *Aristeas* 153, 159; *Spec.* IV 107), they also refer to these regulations as σημεῖα (*Aristeas* 150; *Spec.* IV 106).

[23] This is the Stoic definition of joy in contrast to pleasure. See Colson's note.

Judaism along with other religions during the Hellenistic period was under attack from the side of philosophers of religion for its adherence to much that appeared external in worship instead of a "reasonable worship." The Stoic Posidonius praised Moses for having instituted a pure worship without images among the Jews. But Moses' superstitious successors corrupted this pure worship by adding such practices as circumcision and the dietary regulations.[24] The Biblical cultic legislation relating to the temple, sacrifices, and the priesthood had also come under censure in Hellenism. We recall Hecataeus of Abdera's charge of "superstition" against Jewish rites and practices.[25] Plutarch also said:

> Therefore the longing after divinity is the longing after truth, especially when the truth concerning the gods is the aim; and to possess that all our studies and inquiries are devoted to the acquisition of holiness, a work more holy than religious ceremonies and temple service can be (*De Is.* 351E).

Reitzenstein concludes it is impossible to trace the general Hellenistic attitude that the true cult is a continual praise of God, or that the proper sacrifice is a prayer of thanks, to a single source.[26] The terms $\lambda o \gamma \iota \varkappa \grave{\eta} \; \lambda \alpha \tau \varrho \epsilon \iota \alpha$ (Rom. 12.1) and $\pi \nu \epsilon \upsilon \mu \alpha \tau \iota \varkappa \grave{\alpha} \varsigma \; \vartheta \upsilon \sigma \iota \alpha \varsigma$ (1 Pet. 2.5) seem to be general formulas in Hellenistic theology.[27]

That God has no need of sacrifices was, of course, a consistent teaching of the O.T. prophets (Is. 40.16; Hos. 6.6; Mic. 6.6–8; 1 Sam. 15.22) which Philo repeats (*QE* II 50; *Immut.* 56). But with his faith in the inerrant Torah, Philo was not free to simply reject the ancestral sacrificial institutions as some of the Hebrew prophets may have done and as many Greek philosophers certainly did. Like the Qumran sectaries who, because of their passionate adherence to the Scriptures, desired on the one hand to reconcile the strictures of the prophets against formalistic ritual

---

[24] M. Pohlenz, *Die Stoa* I, p. 212f.

[25] See above p. 43 n. 30.

[26] *Die hellenistischen Mysterienreligionen*, p. 38.

[27] See *ibid.*, p. 328f. for Hermetic parallels. To these can be added the mention in *Test. Levi* 3.6 of a "reasonable fragrance of a bloodless offering" and the fragment of Porphyrius, Eusebius *Praep. Evang.* 4.13, according to which we ought not to sacrifice to the Highest God, "for he needs nothing." God asks instead for our minds, the best in us; one is therefore "under no circumstances to sacrifice to the greatest God exhalted above all."

on the other hand with Scripture's ordinances for sacrifices,[28] Philo looked in the sacrificial rites for symbols of deeper spiritual truths, but now to show that Judaism's sacrifices were more than superstition. It is not for nothing, says Philo, that the instructions for the holy rites in Lev. 2.1f. begin, "If a soul bring a gift or sacrifice." This means that the "server of the sacrifice should be an unbodied soul," not an earthly mortal body performing external rites,[29] for the soul alone can truly pray, give thanks, and offer sacrifice without blemish (*Som.* II 71f.). Therefore the offering of fine flour the text refers to is "the symbol of a will, purified by the councils of instruction, fit to produce nourishment that gives no sickness and life that knows no guilt." The oil and frankincense there refer to the soul being offered, "rich with fatness," that is, "brimful of truths of all sincerity and purity," and "gladdened by light divine and perfumed with the breaths exhaled from justice and other virtues" (*Som.* II 73f.). In Lev. 2.14 we are instructed to make first fruit cereal offerings of new, roasted, sliced, and ground grain. This is really an injunction to accept the new Sophia of God as it springs up in the soul, and which knowledge displaces the old traditions and folklore of mankind (*Sac.* 76–79). The *roasting* of the grain refers to the hardening of the soul with the power of reason so that it is not loose but solid. The *slicing* means that the reason of the soul is to distinguish between the different virtues so that it may "undertake willing service to them both severally and together" (*Sac.* 82–84). The *grinding* of the grain implies that what the mind has grasped must afterward be practiced and exercised persistently so that Virtue's heavenly word may be more firmly impressed upon it (*Sac.* 86f.). Philo says that when all these things are carried out, "you will bring an offering of the first-fruits, even the first and best offering of the soul" (*Sac.* 87).

No point would be served in further multiplying such examples of spiritualized sacrificial legislation which are found throughout Philo's writings.[30] He gives a basis for his spiritualization of sacrifice first by echoing the protest of the prophets and philosophers, "God does not rejoice in sacrifices even if one offer heca-

---

[28] J. Carmignac, "L'utilité ou l'inutilité des sacrifices sanglants dans la 'Règle de la Communaute' de Qumran," *RB*, 1956, p. 530f. See such passages as 1 *QS* IX 3–5 and *Dam.* 11.20f.

[29] Perfunctory sacrifice is "display of external (ἐκτὸς) luxuries" in *Det.* 21.

[30] *On the Sacrifices of Abel and Cain* overflows with them.

tombs, for all things are His possessions" (*Spec.* I 271; cf. *Plant.* 164). Therefore if the worshippers bring no other offering than themselves they make the best of sacrifices to God (*Spec.* I 272; cf. *Plant.* 108; *Mos.* II 107f.).[31] That this is no invention of Philo's own is indicated in the Law itself which specifies that two altars are to be constructed. The one built of stone in the open air is for blood-offerings of beasts, but the one of gold set in the inner shrine is to be used for frankincense offerings. Stone is obviously inferior in worth to gold; therefore the inward offering of the rational spirit (πνεῦμα λογικὸν), symbolized by the golden altar which is in the inner shrine, is more precious to God than the many animals immolated at the outer altar (*Spec.* I 273–277).

---

[31] Cf. Philo's description of the Essenes, "They have shown themselves especially devout in the service of God, not by offering sacrifices of animals, but by resolving to sanctify their minds" (*Prob.* 75). Josephus mentions that the Essenes did not sacrifice in the temple (*Ant.* 18.15). The question of whether the Essenes rejected temple sacrifices in the present age is not answered by the Qumran texts. See O. Cullmann, "The Significance of the Qumran Texts for Research into the Beginnings of Christianity," JBL, 1955, p. 217. Aristeas defines the highest glory as, "Honoring God, and this not in offerings nor in sacrifices but in purity of soul and holy resolution" (234). The conclusion of Aristeas and Philo that the consecration of the inward soul is the only real sacrifice necessary seems to be the consequence of tendencies toward spiritualization of the cult in Judaism plus the contact of Diaspora Judaism with Hellenistic antagonism toward all sacrifice and religious ceremony. As the Jerusalem temple became increasingly inaccessible for the greatest number of Jews, the individual Jew was urged to make his heart and soul a temple for God, his prayers a sacrificial service to him, and his Scripture study a service of the altar. See H. Strack and P. Billerbeck, *Kommentar zum Neuen Testament aus Talmud und Midrash*, Munich, 1924f., II, p. 437, III, pp. 26, 296; G. F. Moore, *Judaism in the First Centuries of the Christian Era* II, Cambridge, 1927, pp. 217f., 240. But the Aristeas-Philo assertion that the consecration of the soul is the *only* offering that matters — one which temple offerings can at best hint at allegorically, seems to go beyond Judaism's attempts at substitution of good works and piety for sacrifice and ends close to Hellenism's radical rejection of it. See I. Heinemann, *Philons griechische und jüdische Bildung*, p. 66f., who points out that Philo never cites the prophets in support of this spiritualizing of the cult.

CHAPTER IV

The Symbolism of the Sanctuary

1: The Temple Apology

As in the case of animal sacrifices, Hellenism had questioned the validity of building temples "made with hands" ($\chi\varepsilon\iota\rho o\pi o\acute{\iota}\eta\tau o\varsigma$).[1] Zeno followed Plato's assertion that in the prehistoric Golden Age there had been no temple made with hands, for hands can never build a house worthy of divinity.[2] Plutarch said:

> For the universe is a most holy temple and most worthy of a god; into it man is introduced through birth as a spectator, not of hand-made or immovable images, but of those sensible representations of knowable things that the divine mind, says Plato, has revealed . . .[3]

Xerxes considered it a fault to confine gods within temples, for the whole world is their house, therefore he ordered the Athenian temples burned.[4]

Philo repeats this repudiation of temples when he asks, what house one should prepare for God, "Shall it be of stone or timber? Away with the thought" (*Cher.* 100). These words, of course, cannot be pressed to mean that Philo objected to Judaism's temple

---

[1] It is worth mentioning that the Hellenist, Stephen, first attacks the institution of sacrifices (Acts 7.43f.), and then the temple "made with hands" (7.48–50). Paul repeats the anti-temple point in 17.48. The Jewish writer of *Sibylline Oracles* rejects temple and sacrifice in the same breath: "Happy shall those men be throughout the earth who . . . when they see them, shall disown all temples and altars, vain erections of senseless stones, befouled with constant blood of living things and sacrifices of four-footed beatsts" (IV 24–30).

[2] M. Pohlenz, *Die Stoa* I p. 137.

[3] *De tranquillitate animi* 477 C, tr. by W. C. Helmbold, The Loeb Classical Library, London, 1939.

[4] Cicero, *Rep.* III 14; F. F. Bruce, *The Acts of the Apostles*, London, p. 336, quotes Euripides, fragment 968: "What house made by workmen could enclose the divine form by layers of walls?

in Jerusalem, to which he paid homage himself (*Prov.* 2.64).[5] For Philo there are two temples, besides the one in Jerusalem. One is the universe, as the Hellenists claimed, and the other is the rational soul (*Som.* I 215). So also when the Lord in Ex. 25.7 (LXX) commands a sanctuary to be made for him, besides meaning the literal tabernacle of Israel, the two tabernacles of world and purified soul are also referred to (*QE* II 51; *Plant.* 50; *Her.* 75).

To show a justification for the existence of the temple Philo proceeds to treat it just as he does sacrifices—he spiritualizes it, showing by allegory what profound intentions lie in its components. The allegory of the temple was evidently a tradition in the apology of the Hellenistic Jews. Non-Jewish critics saw in the temple an instance of Jewish parochialism. How is it that the Jews maintain a localized temple for a God whose universe is his temple? Hence Josephus, who said of the Jerusalem temple, "a better temple than this is the world" (*Bell.* V 458), prefaces his remarks on the symbolism of the Jewish sanctuary by saying:

> But one may well be astonished at the hatred men have for us and which they have so persistently maintained, from an idea that we slight the divinity whom they themselves profess to venerate. For if one reflects on the construction of the tabernacle and looks at the vestments of the priest and the vessels which we use for the sacred ministry, he will discover that our lawgiver was a man of God and that these blasphemous charges against us by the rest of men are idle. In fact, every one of these objects is intended to recall and represent the universe, as he will find if he will but consent to examine them without prejudice and with understanding.[6]

In the passage following and in *Ant.* III 123 and *Bell.* V 212f. Josephus discusses the world's symbolism in the holy sanctuary which Philo carries out at length.

Philo wants to demonstrate that Judaism is not at all a nationalistic religion, but instead a universal religion for all mankind; and this universalism is expressed in its cult. Its sacrifices are not just in behalf of the Jewish nation, but "for all mankind" (*Spec.* I 168; 190).[7] The complaint of the critics that the Jewish temple artificially binds the worship of a presumably universal God to a

---

[5] Nor was he indifferent to it, for Gaius' plan to erect a statue of himself in it amounted to "outraging the splendor of the temple" (*Legat.* 198).

[6] *Ant.* III 180, tr. H. St. J. Thackeray, Loeb Classical Library, London, 1930.

[7] Judaism's feasts have universal meaning as well as national. So the Sabbath "is the festival, not of a single city or country, but of the universe"

particular locality simply is not so. For the Jewish temple is designed according to the structure of the world that men may look at it and know that the world is God's temple. Philo admits that the highest and πρὸς ἀλήθειαν temple of God is the universe. But, he says, there is also a temple "made with hands" in Jerusalem. Philo feels that this temple was erected as a kind of concession to the "pious urge" of mankind which expresses itself in men's desire to offer sacrifices for thanksgiving and to ask for forgiveness of sins.[8] So the priests correspond to God's angels, the votive ornaments to the stars, and the Holy of Holies to the heavens (*Spec.* I 66f.).

Since the descriptions of Solomon's temple (1 Kn. 6; 2 Chron. 3–4) as well as Herod's are not found in the Pentateuch, Philo, with his consistent preference for the Torah, uses its specifications of the tabernacle to lay out the holy cosmic symbolism (*Spec.* I 75–77, see Colson's note). Moses was given instructions for the tabernacle to be constructed to resemble the temple (Ex. 26. 1–14), "a temple made with hands." Its colors were picked to correspond to the basic cosmic elements, earth, water, air, and fire (*Mos.* II 88f.; *Cong.* 116f.). The altar of incense was placed in the middle, symbolic of earth and water "since the mid-position in the universe has been assigned to them" (*Mos.* II 101). Again, it symbolizes the elements in that its wood is of earth, its incense of water, its perfume of air, and the part which is ignited of fire. The elements of the world are also symbolized in the ingredients of the incense (*Her.* 226; 197). Even the animal world is represented in the holy table, for "loaves and libations, which creatures needing food must use, are placed on it" (*Her.* 226), a symbolism which Josephus follows as well (*Bell.* V 217). The candlestick was placed in the south to depict the southern movements of the sun, moon, and other astral bodies; and its seven lamps and candlebearers sym-

---

(*Opif.* 89). The Feast of Unleavened Bread is "in agreement with the general cosmic order" (*Spec.* II 150). Philo explains, "The Jewish nation is to the whole inhabited world what the priest is to the state" (*Spec.* II 163), for it "has received the gift of prophecy and priesthood on behalf of all mankind" (*Abr.* 98). He hoped by such reasoning to refute the charge made by certain people (such as Hecataeus of Abdera, see I. Heinemann, *Philons jüdische und griechische Bildung*, p. 453) that the Jews were characterized by "misanthropy" (*Spec.* II 167; *Virt.* 141).

[8] In *Her.* 112 he declares that God gave the holy tabernacle "in pity for our race."

bolize the planets around the sun (*Mos.* II 102f; *QE* II 75–78; *Her.* 221–225), an interpretation also known by Josephus (*Ant.* III 182; *Bell.* V 217).

A more expanded cosmological allegory of the sanctuary in Ex. 25 appears in *QE* II. The wave or molding around the ark refers to the stars which roll through the heavens (55). The ark's table is of pure gold to show that the world's substance is tested and chosen (69). The lampstand, symbolizing heaven and the planets, is "turned" and of pure gold because heaven turns in its periodic revolutions and is made of a superior fifth element called "the quintessence," indicated by gold (73). The bowls of the lampstand's branches, modelled like nuts, balls, and lilies, stand (1) for the zodiacal signs which are anticipations of coming things like the bud of a nut anticipates the flower, (2) for the spherical shape of heavenly bodies, (3) for the luminousness of the stars like the whiteness of a lily (76). The lampstand gives light only in one direction, indicating that the planets do not move in every part of the celestial sphere, but only in the southern region (79). The veil in the sanctuary which separates the holy and divine things inside from the lesser things outside symbolizes the separation between the unchanging heavenly region of the universe and the lower parts of the cosmos subject to change (91). Both Josephus and Philo assert that the colors of its tapestries denote the four basic elements of Nature: white stands for earth, purple for water, blue for air, and scarlet for fire (*QE* II 85, 92; *Mos.* II 88; *Cong.* 116f.; *Ant.* III 183; *Bell.* V 212–214).

2: The Allegory of the High Priest and His Clothing

One feature of the cosmological apology of the Hellenistic Jews for their temple was the interpretation of the high priest and his clothing. Like the rest of the ornaments of the temple the high priest's garments also represent the world. Josephus continues his arguments against the detractors of Judaism by stating that the high priest's garments also have universal symbolism:

> The high-priest's tunic likewise signifies the earth, being of linen, and its blue the arch of heaven, while it recalls the lightening by its pomegranates, the thunder by the sound of its bells.[9]

---

[9] *Ant.* III 184; Thackeray's tr.

Josephus follows this with more interpretation of the high priest's clothing which agrees in one detail with Philo's high priest allegory which like Josephus' is based on Ex. 28 (*Mos.* II 117–135). Both writers agree that the stones around the priest's neck represent the zodiac circle (*Ant.* III 186; *Mos.* II 124–126), and Philo mentions "some think" that the two emerald stones on the shoulder pieces symbolize the sun and moon (*Mos.* II 122), which happens to be Josephus' opinion (*Ant.* III 187), although Philo himself prefers a different interpretation. Although both writers have interjected personal preferences in the high priest allegory, it is clear that they are passing on a Jewish thought original to neither of them.[10] Philo states that the high priest is so bedecked in order that the whole universe (the real temple of God) may pictorially enter the sanctuary with him when he sacrifices and prays (*Mos.* II 131). So *Wisdom of Solomon* declares that Moses was able to intercede for the people of Israel as high priest, "For upon his long robe the whole world was depicted" (18.24).

At the end of another long passage on the cosmic symbols of the high priest's dress (*Spec.* I 84–97), Philo says clearly what the universal religious significance of the garments is:

> Among the other nations the priests are accustomed to offer prayers and sacrifices for their kinsmen and friends and fellow-countrymen only, but the high priest of the Jews makes prayers and gives thanks not only on behalf of the whole human race but also for the parts of nature, earth, water, air, fire. For he holds the world to be, as in very truth it is, his country, and in its behalf he is wont to propitiate the Ruler with supplication and intercession, beseeching Him to make His creature a partaker of His own kindly and merciful nature (*Spec.* I 97).

Further he says that to the high priest

> it has been committed to wear the aforesaid tunic, which is a copy and replica of the whole heaven, the intention of this being that the universe may join with man in the holy rites and man with the universe (*Som.* I 215).

Of all the religions of the world, only Judaism deserves to be called universal, a fact borne out by the world symbolism of its

---

[10] Levi is told in a vision to "put on the robe of the priesthood, and the crown of righteousness, and the breastplate of understanding, and the garment of truth, and the plate of faith, and the turban of the head, and the ephod of prophecy" (*Test. Levi* 8.2). This interpretation of the priesthood garments is, of course, totally different from Philo's and Josephus', but shows how even Pharisaism was finding profound symbolism in the priestly clothing.

temple and the dress and services of the priests who pray and sacrifice in it.[11]

We cannot leave this discussion without noting the Logos symbolism of Philo's allegory of the high priest. Nowhere in the treatises of the writings called the *Exposition of the Law*, which were apologies written for Gentiles,[12] does Philo mention that the high priest as mediator represents the divine Logos between God and the world.[13] This symbolism is worked out instead in the *Allegorical Commentary*, written for Jews, and therefore did not play a part in his cosmological apology to the Gentiles which we have just looked at. But this does not mean that the high priest's Logos symbolism in his writings for Jewish readers did not fulfill an apologetic function too. Addressing Hellenistically educated Jews in the temptation of apostasy from Judaism,[14] Philo needed to show the profound spiritual meanings of the cult to his own people as well.

Among his many statements about the Logos as a divine hypostasis, Philo notes that it is neither uncreated as God, nor created as man,[15] but a mediator ($\mu\acute{\epsilon}\sigma\sigma\varsigma$) and surety (*Her.* 206), interceding for both:

---

[11] F. Geiger, *op. cit.*, p. 105 n. 66, finds behind *Spec.* I 97 the Stoic idea of the cosmopolis. But I think a parallel with more religious similarly to Philo's apology of the high priest's clothing is the vision Lucius has of Isis. Isis is clothed with many articles resembling parts of the cosmos, and she says of her universal cult: "My name, my divinity is adored throughout all the world, in divers manners, in variable customs, and by many names ... Therefore be ready and attentive to my commandment; the day which shall come after this night is dedicated to my service by an eternal religion;" *Apuleius the Golden Ass*, XI 4–5, tr. W. Adlington, revised by S. Gaselee, The Loeb Classical Library, London, 1935. See J. Paschar, *He Basilike Hodos, Der Königsweg zu Wiedergeburt und Vergöttung bei Philo von Alexandreia (Studien zur Geschichte und Kultur des Altertums)*, Paderborn, 1931, pp. 48 to 60, for a discussion of the similarity between Philo's priestly garment allegory and the symbolic interpretation of the clothing of gods in Plutarch, Apuleius, and the Hermetic literature.

[12] E. Goodenough, "Philo's Exposition of the Law and his De Vita Mosis," *The Harvard Theological Review*, 1933, pp. 109–124.

[13] In *Mos.* II 125 ff. the λογεῖον, breast-plate (see Ex. 28.15 LXX), of the high priest is taken to represent the Logos who "holds together and administers all things." In *QE* II 110–117 it represents human reason, except at the end in a passage re-worked by a Christian scribe; cf. *Mos.* II 127.

[14] See above p. 21.

[15] A Greek fragment of *QG* II 62 refers to the Logos as "the second God."

To His Word, His chief messenger highest in age and honour, the Father of all has given the special prerogative, to stand on the border and separate the creature from the Creator. This same Word both pleads with the immortal as suppliant (ἱκέτης) for afflicted mortality and acts as ambassador of the ruler to the subject (*Her.* 205).

Philo remarks that this intercessory function of the Logos parallels that of the Jewish high priest, and therefore on one occasion says, "If again you examine the High Priest, the Logos . . ." (*Mig.* 102), to introduce an allegory of the garments. In the mediating of the high priest the mediating of the universal Logos is portrayed, for the Logos occupies the world and operates in it like the high priest in the temple (*Som.* I 215). Like the Logos whom he symbolizes, the high priest stands on the borderline between God and man, for through him men have a mediator (μέσος) through whom they may propitiate God, just as God has in him an agent through whom his boons are given to mankind because the priest has "a nature higher than the merely human . . . approximate to the Divine" (*Spec.* I 116). When Philo speaks in this way it seems clear that his Logos allegory of the high priest has affected his view of the priest's own person, so that the high priest in some sense was attributed qualities of the Logos which he represented, thus becoming for Philo a quasi-divine figure.[16] Therefore Philo says of the high priest in the verse, "When he enters into the holy of holies he will not be a man[17] until he comes out:"

> And if he then becomes no man, clearly neither is he God, but God's minister, through the mortal in him in affinity with creation, through the immortal with the uncreated, and he retains this μέσην τάξιν until he comes out again to the realm of body and flesh (*Som.* II 231f.).

Lev. 16.17 also teaches that the high priest actually shares both the nature of God and man, "as it were, one his head, the other his feet" (*Som.* II 189).

---

[16] So H. Wenschkewitz, *Die Spiritualisierung der Kultusbegriffe, Tempel, Priester, und Opfer im Neuen Testament*, Leipzig, 1932, p. 73. S. Belkin, *Philo and the Oral Law*, Cambridge, Mass., 1940, p. 79, claims it is dangerous to confuse the allegorist Philo with Philo the expounder of the Jewish laws, and therefore refuses to consider the allegorical Logos symbolism in his treatment of the high priest in Philo. However I hope this presentation shows that Philo, here as in other instances, does not always keep his literal and mystical interpretation separate, and one has influenced the other.

[17] Lev. 16.17 LXX, or, "a man shall not be there . . ."

The high priest's half divine nature makes possible his being free from sin (*Spec.* I 243), since absolute sinlessness is a property of God alone, or of the ϑεῖος ἀνήρ (*Virt.* 177). The provision for the priest's making atonement for his involuntary sins, bringing guilt to the whole nation (Lev. 4.3), Philo twists around to mean that the high priest himself is immune from sin and that if he makes a slip it is always something forced on him by the collective sin of the nation (*Spec.* I 230; cf. *Spec.* III 134).

3: The Inward Temple and High Priest

The temple and high priest were also spiritualized in another way mentioned in texts at the beginning of this discussion.[18] Once more to show that the rites and priesthood of the Jewish temple were not simply religious externalism, Philo emphasized that the cosmic truths depicted in the temple and high priest apply as well in the world of the human soul, since he accepts the Greek theory that men and the universe stand in the relation of microcosm to macrocosm (*Opif.* 82; *Mos.* II 135).[19]

> For there are, as is evident, two temples of God; one of them this universe, in which there is also as High Priest His First-born, the divine Word, and the other the rational soul, whose Priest is the real Man; the outward and visible image of whom is he who offers the prayers and sacrifices handed down from our fathers. (*Som.* I 215; so *Her.* 75)

He gives the etymology "vision of peace" to the name Jerusalem, which is only another way of saying "vision of God." Therefore the vision-seeking mind not made of wood and stone is the holiest house of God and "may justly be called the dwelling-place and city of God" (*Som.* II 250–253). So Philo admonishes his soul to be zealous to become a house of God, a holy temple in which the Lord may dwell (*QE* II 51; *Som.* I 149), for God finds no temple worthier than the reasoning faculty of man (*Virt.* 188). In this temple of the soul, the rational faculty corresponds to the high priest in the temple and his functions. Just as the high priest

---

[18] See above p. 55 f.

[19] An idea Galen attributes to "men of old" in general; see E. Goodenough, "A Neo-Pythagorean Source in Philo Judaeus," *Yale Classical Studies,* 1932, p. 129 f.

is the convener of the holy congregation, so the rational faculty of the soul is the chairman, president, and chief magistrate without whom the soul's parts could never be convened (*Som.* II 187). When Moses functioning as high priest poured the blood into the mixing bowls (Ex. 24.6), our irrational senses are signified by the bowls which should be made alive (blood is taken as the principle of life here) to follow "the divine courses of the mind" (*Her.* 185). The division of the high priest's breast-plate depicts the division of the rational faculty into the λόγος προφορικὸς (speech) and the λόγος ἐνδιάθετος (thought; *Gig.* 52; *Mos.* II 125–130; *QE* II 110–117).

When the high priest enters the holy of holies once a year (Lev. 16. 34; Ex. 28. 35), the mystic heavenward soar of the mind toward divine things is thereby signified (*Som.* II 231–233; *Gig.* 52; *Mig.* 104). As the high priest is about to enter the sacred place the bells of his garment shall be audible (Ex. 28.35). This suggests that during the soul's mystic flight as it is on the point of entering the world of divine and intelligible truths our senses also chime in with the mind in a hymn sung by our whole composite being (*Mig.* 104). Once the mind reaches this heavenly holy of holies, it is to dedicate "the incense of consecrated virtues" (*Som.* II 232; cf. Lev. 16.11–14).

CHAPTER V

The Alexandrian Jewish Background
to the Epistle to the Hebrews

1: The Background Problem

According to Acts 18.24–28 an Alexandrian Jew "well-versed in the scriptures," Apollos, when received into the Christian fellowship, used his Alexandrian Biblical knowledge to advantage: "For he powerfully confuted the Jews in public, showing by the scriptures that the Christ was Jesus." There was a time when it was commonly accepted that the Epistle to the Hebrews was written by one whose origins were in Alexandrian Judaism of the kind represented by Philo. The history of exegesis shows ample conjectures that Apollos of Alexandria was the author of Heb.[1] But in the last two or three decades attempts have been made to find another background for the epistle. E. F. Scott,[2] while affirming a similarity between elements in Philo and Heb., also brought forth the idea that the epistle showed certain affinities with the speech of Stephen (Acts 7) and therefore proposed that the letter came from one in Stephen's circle called "the Hellenists" (Acts 6.1). This idea, subsequently denied by J. Moffatt,[3] a few years ago was made the basic thesis of W. Manson's study.[4] The effect of his work was to shift the background of the epistle away from Alexandrianism, which he felt had been much exaggerated in scholarship,[5] while he interpreted the letter as expressing the mission theology of Stephen's group.[6]

---

[1] F. Lobue, "The Historical Background of the Epistle to the Hebrews," JBL, 1956, pp. 52–57, gives a survey of this theory in modern times.

[2] *The Epistle to the Hebrews: Its Doctrine and Significance*, Edinburgh, 1923, pp. 62–64.

[3] Commentary, p. lxii.

[4] *The Epistle to the Hebrews*, Edinburgh, 1951.

[5] *Ibid.*, pp. 123 ff.

[6] It seems to me that M. Simon, *St. Stephen and the Hellenists in the Primitive Church*, London, 1958, pp. 100–104, has satisfactorily answered

Another approach was taken by E. Käsemann[7] who used as parallel material to the Christology of Heb. the *Urmensch* myth of various Gnostic texts. He claimed that the expectation of a Messianic high priest prevalent in the days of the Hasmoneans was apparently united with the Gnostic *anthropos* myth and finally came to the idea of the *Urmensch* high priest who offers himself for the sins of the people. The first evidence of this synthesis is in Philo and Heb., although Heb. has not taken this idea from Philo directly. For Käsemann both Heb. and Philo attest to this synthesis independently.[8] But the conceptions of a high priest who is offered for sins, or even the idea of an *Urmensch* high priest, we may say, are totally lacking in Philo.

From his study of the Dead Sea scrolls Y. Yadin[9] came to the tentative conclusion that the addresses of Heb. must have been a group which originally belonged to the Qumran sect, subsequently were converted to Christianity, and brought some of their previous beliefs with them. Two years later H. Kosmala carried this idea to the point of saying that Heb. was written to a group of Essenes like the Qumran community which were still Jews.[10]

Manson, showing that the differences between Stephen's speech and Heb. outweigh the similarities. If a connection is ever to be made between Heb. and the Stephen group it will not be done through such a problematic source as Acts 7, but through the Johannine literature which evidently stands in the Hellenist tradition; cf. O. Cullmann, "A New Approach to the Interpretation of the Fourth Gospel," ET, 1959, pp. 8–11; 34–42.

[7] *Das wandernde Gottesvolk,*[2] Göttingen, 1957.

[8] *Ibid.,* p. 140 *et passim.*

[9] "The Dead Sea scrolls and the Epistle to the Hebrews," *Scripta Hierosolymitana* 4, Jerusalem, 1957.

[10] *Hebräer-Essener-Christen, Studien zur Vorgeschichte der frühchristlichen Verkündigung,* Leiden, 1959. When Kosmala (p. 89) is forced to admit that the Greek of the letter indicates that the *Umgangssprache* of the readers was Greek, and that they lived in a Greek-speaking area outside Palestine, it seems to me he completely undermines his whole thesis. There is no evidence that the Essene movement was so widespread as this; cf. Josephus *Bell.* II 8.2–13; Philo *Prob.* 75, *Apo.* 11.1. Furthermore Kosmala assumes throughout that the writer was thoroughly familiar with the Essene Hebrew backgrounds of the Greek terms he uses; cf. for instance his explanation of the term "apostle" (Heb. 3.1), pp. 77ff. From the writer of Heb.'s complete dependence upon the LXX (see above p. 83f.) and his un-Hebrew understanding of words such as $\delta\iota\alpha\vartheta\acute{\eta}\varkappa\eta$ (9.16–17), we may conclude that he never read a Hebrew text. It is therefore futile to think he knew what the equivalents of his terms were and meant in any Hebrew literature.

C. Spicq has recently devoted a special section in his commentary[11] demonstrating once more that Philo affords the best Jewish background source for the study of the epistle. Since many would find dubious some evidence adduced by Spicq, it seems necessary that a special part of this study be given to establish what is here a basic point – namely, that the writer of Heb. has come from the same school of Alexandrian Judaism as Philo, and that Philo's writings still offer us the best single body of *religionsgeschichtlich* material we have for this N.T. document.

2: Common Text

There are the following LXX readings which are attested only in Philo and Heb.: Gen. 2.2, καὶ κατέπαυσεν ὁ θεὸς ἐν τῇ ἡμέρᾳ κ.τ.λ., *Post.* 64; Heb. 4.4; LXX: καὶ κατέπαυσεν τῇ ἡμέρα κ.τ.λ., Josh. 1.5: οὐ μή σε ανῶ οὐδ' μή σε ἐγκαταλίπω, *Conf.* 166; Heb. 13.5; LXX: οὐκ ἐγκαταλείπω σε οὐδὲ ὑπερόψομαι σε. This plus the fact that Heb. follows the Codex Alexandrinus[12] seems to indicate a geographical proximity of both writers.

3: Reflections of the Philonic Doctrine of the Logos

In Heb. and particularly in the prologue certain Philonic statements about the Logos have been applied to the Son. The Son is the reflection (ἀπαύγασμα, only here in the Bible) of the divine glory (1.3). Philo says that everyone, so far as his mind is concerned, is like the Logos, an ἀπαύγασμα of God, "the blessed Nature" (*Opif.* 146). The Son is χαρακτὴρ of the divine essence (1.3). Compare with this Philo's doctrine that man's spirit is stamped by the seal of God, "the χαρακτὴρ of which is the eternal Logos" (*Plant.* 18). The Son is the one "through whom (δἰ οὗ) God made the world" (1.2; 3.3,4).[13] Similarly *Cher.* 127 says, the world's cause is God, "and its instrument is the Logos of God through

---

[11] pp. 39–91.

[12] P. Padva, *Les citations de l'Ancien Testament dans l'Épître aux Hébreux*, Paris, 1904, p. 33, and E. Riggenbach's commentary, xxxiv, xxxv.

[13] See as well, "Jesus Christ, δἰ οὗ all things were made," 1 Cor. 8.6, and Jn. 1.3; Col. 1.16.

whom (δι' οὖ) it was built." Heb. 11.3 states, "The world was created by the Word of God (ῥῆμα θεοῦ), and *Sac.* 8 says that Moses was translated through the Word (ῥῆμα) of God "even through that Word by which (δι' οὖ) also the whole universe was formed." *Spec.* I 81 reads: "And the image of God is the Word through whom (δι' οὖ) the whole universe was framed." Heb. 1.3 asserts the Son "bears the universe (φέρων τε τὰ πάντα) by the word of his power."[14] *Plant.* 8 says, "No material thing is so strong as to be able to bear the burden of the world (τὸν κόσμον ἀχθοφορεῖν); ... the everlasting Word of the eternal God is the very sure and staunch prop of the whole." The odd idiom[15] φέρειν τὰ πάντα is paralleled also in Philo's thought on God's creative sustenance of the cosmos: πάντα φέρων σπουδαῖα ὁ θεὸς (*Mut.* 256). The N.T. title "Son" used so often in Heb. is not without parallel to the Logos in Philo, called πρωτόγονος υἱός (*Som.* I 215; *Agr.* 51), and πρεσβύτατος (*Her.* 205; *Conf.* 146; *LA* III 175).[16]

In Heb. the Logos of God is

living and active, sharper than any two-edged sword, piercing to the division of soul and spirit, of joints and marrow, and discerning the thoughts and intentions of the heart. And before him no creature is hidden, but all are open and laid bear to the eyes of him with whom we have to do. (4.12–13)

The comparison of the Word of God to a sword appears in the Midrash[17] as well as in Jewish apocalyptic literature,[18] and is found in Eph. 6.17. The Biblical uniqueness of this passage is the thought that the Logos of God has a function of penetrating man to convict (κριτικὸς) "the thoughts and deliberations of the heart." The λόγος τομεὺς (*Her.* 225) doctrine found in Philo readily explains these verses. In *Her.* 129–236 Philo explains that the Logos is the divider of all creation. In the creation of the world the Logos divided Being into heavy and light, then into the elements earth, fire, air, and water, and into all the further subdivisions. "Thus God sharpened the edge of his all-cutting Word,

---

[14] Cf. Col. 1.17.

[15] See Colson's note at *Her.* 36: ὁ τὰ μή ὄντα φέρων καὶ τὰ πάντα γεννῶν.

[16] The name "Son of God" is also applied to the Logos in the Hermetic literature; see C. H. Dodd, *The Bible and the Greeks*, London, 1935, pp. 117ff.

[17] See Strack-Billerbeck.

[18] See Windisch, commentary.

and divided universal being" (140). Like the Ephor Dike[19] the Logos "... also has keenest sight, and is able to survey (ἐφορᾶν) all things" (*LA* III 171). The cutting Word of God also is like a sword which lances and probes the hidden thoughts of men. So Phinehas the priest is praised for he took the lance,

> that is, the sharp-edged λόγος able to probe and explore each thing... that duped by none and armed with mighty strength he should pierce passion [the Medianite woman] through the womb. (*Mut.* 108; Num. 25.8)

Philo identifies the fiery sword in the Garden of Eden as a symbol of the Logos (*Cher.* 28, 30), and says further,

> For he that opens the womb of each of these, of mind, to mental apprehensions, of speech, to the activities of the voice, of the senses, to receive the pictures presented to it by objects, of the body, to the movements and postures proper to it, is the invisible, seminal artificer, the divine Word (*Her.* 119).

As in Heb. 4.12 the Logos penetrates to the soul and judges the thoughts of the heart, likewise the Logos entered the soul of Abimelech and took Sarah (Gen. 20.3):

> The foolish man ... is convicted by the divine Logos, which enters his soul and examines and searches him and forces him to confess that this is the possession of another man and not his (*QG* IV 62; cf. III 23).

C. Spicq[20] has also explained the phrase where the Logos pierces "to the division of soul and spirit" as an expression of Philonic anthropology. Philo needed to reconcile Lev. 17.11, "the spirit of all flesh is the blood," according to which the essence of the soul is blood, and Gen. 2.7, "And he breathed into his face the breath of life, and man became a living soul," according to which the soul's essence is spirit. So he says the soul is divided into an animal and a rational principle. The animal principle we share with the beasts; but the origin and fountain of the rational principle is God. Blood is the essence of the first, and spirit is the essence of the second (*Det.* 82). At another passage he says:

> We use "soul" in two senses, both for the whole soul and also for its dominant part, which properly speaking is the soul's mind, just as the eye can mean either the whole orb, or the most important part, by which we see. And therefore the lawgiver held that the substance of the soul

---

[19] See *Dec.* 95, 177; *Prob.* 89.
[20] Commentary I, pp. 52f.

twofold, blood being that of the soul as a whole, and the divine breath or spirit that of its most dominant part. (*Her.* 55; cf. *Mig.* 3)

Heb. is evidently referring to the cleavage in the soul into which in Philo's thinking the Logos penetrates till it reaches the "soul's soul," whose essence is spirit.

Heb. 6.5, "having tasted the good Word of God (ῥῆμα ϑεοῦ)," unique in the Bible, is also a Philonic expression. Compare to it *Fug.* 137, 138:

> Being learners they found the Word of God and divine Logos (ῥῆμα ϑεοῦ καὶ λόγον ϑεῖον) from which all instructions and wisdoms flow eternally . . . They see it and taste it (γευσάμεναι) and are filled with pleasure."

Certainly some of Heb.'s statements we have noted in this paragraph can be paralleled with similar thoughts in other N.T. passages. But as we gather them altogether and compare them with the Logos doctrine in Philo, the evidence becomes preponderant that N.T. parallels are not enough to explain all the ideas here discussed. The Alexandrian Jewish Logos doctrine expressed in Philo must have also been familiar to the writer.

4: The Activities of the High Priest

Heb. 9.7 explains that "the high priest alone goes once a year into the second tent." Here the general thought goes back to Lev. 16, the regulations for the Day of Atonement. This day was celebrated once a year, but on that day the high priest entered the second tent at least three times. After having killed a bull as a sacrifice for himself and his house, first the high priest went into the holy of holies with a censer of coals and two handfuls of incense (vv. 11–13). Next he went out, took some of the bull's blood, came back inside, and sprinkled the mercy seat with it (v. 14). Finally he went back outside, killed a goat as a sin offering for the people, then brought its blood inside again and sprinkled the mercy seat just as he had done with the bull's blood (v. 15). The thought that the high priest went into the holy of holies only once a year (ἅπαξ τοῦ ἐνιαυτοῦ, 9.7) seems to have been a tradition, simplified no doubt for speculation, in Alexandrian Judaism, witnessed to by Philo repeatedly. Of the sanctuary he says, "For all inside is unseen except by the high priest alone, and indeed he, though charged with the duty of entering once a year, gets no view of anything" (*Spec.* I 72; cf. *Ebr.* 136; *Gig.* 52; *Legat.* 306). Contrary to the stipulations in Lev. 16, Philo expressly precludes the high priest's making repeated entrances on the one day per year he officiates in the holy of holies: "Even if the high priest himself enters on two days of the year or on the same day three or four times death without appeal remains his doom" (*Legat.* 307).

Writers are frequently puzzled by Heb. 7.27:

> He has no need, like those high priests, to offer sacrifices daily, first for his own sins and then for those of the people ...

Josephus notes that the high priest officiated with the rest of the priests on the sabbath, at the new moon, at the celebration of the national festivals, or annual solemnities,[21] but there is no evidence outside Philo, Biblical or otherwise, that the high priest offered sacrifices daily.[22] But Philo says that the high priest "day by day offers prayers and sacrifices and asks for blessings ..." (*Spec.* III 131).[23]

5: The Divine Oath

Both Heb. and Philo give the same reason why God in Gen. 22.16 introduces his oath to Abraham saying, "I have sworn by myself": Heb. 6.13: "For when God made a promise to Abraham, since he had no one greater by whom to swear, he swore by himself;" *LA* III 203: "You mark that God swears not by some other thing,

---

[21] *Ant.* III 10.257; *Bell.* V 5.230.

[22] See Spicq.

[23] A. Seeberg, "Versuch einer neuen Erklärung von Hebräer 7.27." *Neue Jahrbücher für deutsche Theologie*, 1894, pp. 368 ff., says that the procedure of the high priest offering once for his own sins and then for the sins of the people shows the writer was thinking of the offerings of the Day of Atonement (Lev. 16.6, 15) which, as he knows (10.1) were offered only once a year. Seeberg insists therefore that the καθ᾽ ἡμέραν be related not to the priests' work at all but to Christ's, and the negation "like those high priests" be referred to the practice of making first one and then another sacrifice. But this explanation leaves unanswered why Christ's work is put in such terms as "each day." There is no inconsistency here with the statement in 10.1 if we see that the writer is not speaking (7.27) of the Day of Atonement at all. But the procedure on the Day of Atonement of offering first for oneself and then for the people has been generalized by the writer so that he thinks this sequence was followed in all sacrificial rites.

for nothing is higher than He, but by Himself, who is best of all things." Then Philo explains that the purpose of God's oath is to assist human faith. For God's swearing is a foundation, assurance, or security for believing:

> An oath is added to assist faith, and only God and one who is God's friend is faithful ... Moreover, the very words of God are oaths and laws of God ... It would seem to be a corollary from this that all God's words are oaths receiving confirmation (βεβαιούμενοι) by accomplishment in act.. God alone therefore is the strongest security (βεβαιωτής) first for Himself, and in the next place for His deeds also, so that He naturally swore by Himself when giving assurance as to himself, a thing impossible for another than He (*LA* III 204; 207; cf. *Abr.* 273).

Thus God's swearing provides the grounds for faith because when God swears there is no longer any room for doubt. Likewise Heb. says that since God wished to provide a foundation for belief to "those who through faith and long-suffering inherit the promises" (6.12), he guaranteed it by means of an oath (ἐμεσίτευσεν ὅρκῳ, v. 17). Now, says Heb., we have a "strong encouragement to seize the hope set before us" (v. 18). Such a hope is like "an anchor of the soul, sure and steadfast (βέβαιος)" (v. 19). Thus both exegetes agree that the purpose of divine swearing in Gen. 22.16 was to guarantee faith.

6: Other Convergences of Philo and Hebrews

When Heb. 10.3 says, "But in these sacrifices there is a reminder of sin year after year," the writer is applying to all sacrificial worshippers the thesis of Philo that "If the worshipper is without kindly feeling or justice, the sacrifices are no sacrifices ... when to outward appearance they are offered, it is not a remission but a reminder of past sins which they effect" (*Mos.* II 107; cf. *Spec.* I 215).

The term Λευιτικός (Heb. 7.11) is not otherwise found in the Bible nor in any Jewish Hellenistic literature, but Philo uses it (*Fug.* 87, 93; *Mut.* 2).

In Heb. 11.10 Abraham "expected a city with foundations. The builder and maker of it was to be God." The detail that Abraham was looking for a city made by God is lacking in Genesis according to which Abraham migrated expecting the promised land of

Canaan as his inheritance (cf. 12.5–7). But Philo calls the land promised to Abraham a "city":

> What good thing had Abram already done, that he bids him estrange himself from fatherland and kindred there and dwell in whatever land God Himself may give him? And that is a city good and large and very prosperous, for great and precious are God's gifts. (*LA* III 83)

Philo's meaning is that the departure of Abraham from Ur and his migration to Canaan symbolizes the mind which "in its desire to improve itself seeks to change its abode for a better one" (*ibid.*, 84).

The following statement in Heb. 11.10, that the builder ($\tau\varepsilon\chi\nu\iota\tau\eta\varsigma$) and maker ($\delta\eta\mu\iota\upsilon\upsilon\rho\gamma\grave{o}\varsigma$) of the city is God, is likewise unique in the Bible. Moffatt says, "$\tau\varepsilon\chi\nu\iota\tau\eta\varsigma$ is not a LXX term, and only began to be used of God in Alexandrian Judaism (e.g. in Wis. 13.1)." God is never called the Demiurge in the Bible outside Heb. 11.10, and the reason for this is not far to seek. For in its secular usage "Demiurge" often referred to a second God who created the material world.[24] Philo says of the creative power of God: "... through this the Father who is its begetter and contriver ($\acute{o}$ $\gamma\varepsilon\nu\nu\acute{\eta}\sigma\alpha\varsigma$ $\varkappa\alpha\grave{\iota}$ $\tau\varepsilon\chi\nu\iota\tau\varepsilon\acute{\upsilon}\sigma\alpha\varsigma$ $\pi\alpha\tau\acute{\eta}\varrho$) made the universe, so that 'I am thy God' is equivalent to 'I am the Maker' and $\delta\eta\mu\iota\upsilon\upsilon\rho\gamma\acute{o}\varsigma$" (*Mut.* 29; cf. 32). Similarly he declares:

> Just as the great Artificer ($\tau\varepsilon\chi\nu\acute{\iota}\tau\eta\varsigma$) divided our soul and limbs in the middle, so too, when he wrought ($\acute{\varepsilon}\delta\eta\mu\iota\upsilon\acute{\upsilon}\rho\gamma\varepsilon\iota$) the world, did He deal with the being of all that is (*Her.* 133; cf. further *Mut.* 30; *Opif.* 36, 68, 138,139,146).

It seems plain that in 11.10 the writer is using Alexandrian school terminology. When he mentions Abraham's seeking a city made by God, he accidentally or purposely writes a thought firmly impressed upon him, namely that the migration of Abraham represents leaving the material sphere to sojourn to a heavenly intelligible one, to a city of God.

There are other indications in chap. 11 that the writer echoes school tradition found in Philo as well. But this material we will take up later. So many parallels as we have discovered between Philo and Heb. cannot be by chance. Until some source dating

---

[24] In the Hermetic literature as in *Timaeus* 69 C the Demiurge was an offspring of God; see C. H. Dodd, *The Bible and the Greeks*, p. 138.

earlier than the letter is discovered representing many of the things discussed in this chapter plus other uniquenesses found in Heb., it seems best to hold fast to the conclusion reached by many, that the writer of Heb. has come from the Alexandrian school which historically runs from the LXX through *Wisdom of Solomon*, Aristobulus, and the *Letter of Aristeas* to Philo.

7: The Anti-Judaic Debate

Heb. was written to a congregation in danger of falling into apostasy.[25] Some have stated that nowhere in the letter is it indicated that the temptation is apostasy into Judaism, and that the danger is rather a drifting into irreligion.[26] But as A. Oepke[27] notes, the persistent urging in the epistle to hold fast to the faith side by side with the writer's anti-Judaic argument makes no sense if Judaism were not attractive to the readers. Furthermore at 13.9, 10 the writer says:

> Do not be carried away by various and foreign teachings. For it is good that the heart be confirmed by grace, not by foods; for those leading their lives according to such things have not been profited. We have an altar from which those venerating[28] the tabernacle have no right to eat.

The following context makes the point that the readers should spiritualize certain O.T. sacrificial practices.[29] Following the same vein of thought in vv. 9–10 the writer states that externalism in

---

[25] Note the passages including such phrases as: "lest we drift away" (2.1); "if we neglect such a great salvation" (2.3); "if we hold fast ... " (3.6); "in committing apostasy from the living God" (3.12); "that no one may fall by the same kind of disobedience" (4.12); "let us hold fast our confession" (4.14); "if they fall away" (6.6); "not neglecting to meet together" (10.25); "do not throw away your confidence" (10.35); "let us run with perseverance" (12.1); "you are enduring for discipline" (12.7).

[26] So E. Scott, *op. cit.*, pp. 16, 23.

[27] *Das neue Gottesvolk*, Gütersloh, 1950, p. 21.

[28] On this sense of λατρείω in Heb., see below p. 110.

[29] The bodies of the animals burned outside the camp (Lev. 16.27) represent a spiritual truth for the Christians to follow (vv. 11–13); the readers ought to offer to God a sacrifice of praise whose offering fruits are lips confessing God's name (v. 15); doing good and making material contributions amount to well-pleasing sacrifices to God (v. 16).

religion never helped anyone.[30] His reference to the tabernacle makes it abundantly clear that he is throughout placing the old and the new faith side by side. So when he says, "Do not be carried away by various and foreign teachings," he means, "Do not be lead into apostasy by Judaism's doctrines."[31] Heb.'s point that the readers must be prepared to bear ill-treatment and abuse for Christ (12.3–11, 13.13) lets us know that the congregation stood before some imminent persecution. In the Roman world that could only mean the demand of repudiation of the Christian confession under duress by police authorities.[32] Under impending persecution we know that Christians sometimes took refuge in Jewish synagogues,[33] espousing Judaism as a *religio licita*.[34] It is against such renunciations of the new faith and taking flight in the old that the writer is warning the congregation. For if one apostatizes from Christianity once, there is no possibility for a future repentance (6.4–6, 12.16–17, 10.26–29). Heb. is an anti-Judaic epistle in which the writer argues to convince a Christian congregation through an exposition of several O.T. passages that lapse into Judaism is fatal. Our task is to determine to what degree and in what ways this exegesis of the O.T. is influenced by the Alexandrian background of the writer. To do this we will now compare and contrast exegetical methods and conclusions of Heb. with those in Philo, using the latter as our prime specimen of the Alexandrian Jewish school.

---

[30] Cf. the contrast food-grace, v. 9. Spicq's suggestion that "foods" here refer to the eating of sacrificial animals (Lev. 7.6, 10.17f., 19.5–6) seems right.

[31] The terms "strange" or "foreign" doctrines (v. 9) for Judaism does of course seem odd. It may be evidence, as T.W. Manson, "The Problem of the Epistle to the Hebrews," *BJRL*, 1949, p. 12f., and G. Bornkamm, "Das Bekenntnis im Hebräerbrief," *TB*, 1942, c. 62f., think, that the readers were tempted by a kind of Jewish theosophy like that which Paul warns against in Col. 2.16, 21ff. (cf. also I Tim. 1.6–7, 4.3; Tit. 1.13ff.).

[32] Pliny, *Ep.* 10.96.5; *Mart. of Polycarp* 9.3; 1 Cor. 12.3.

[33] Justin, *Dial. with Trypho* 47.5.

[34] G. Bornkamm, *ibid.*, c. 60; A. Seeberg, *Der Brief an die Hebräer*, Leipzig, 1912, p. 3f.

CHAPTER VI

The Christological Fulfillment of Scripture

1: Prophetic Inspiration and Interpretation

Not only did Philo persistently follow the LXX to the exclusion of the Hebrew text, he also imputed divine verbal inspiration to the writers of the Greek text, saying its makers were more hierophants and prophets than translators (*Mos.* II 26–44), whose work differed in no detail whatever from the original. Nowhere does Heb. claim this kind of inspiration for the LXX translators, but he at least accepts the Greek version with the same confidence as Philo did. Several writers have studied the O.T. citations in Heb. and have reached the common opinion that the writer knew and quoted only the LXX.[1] If Paul sometimes corrected his Greek Bible by comparing it with the Hebrew,[2] our writer occasionally bases his arguments on actual mistranslations in his text,[3] just as

---

[1] F. Harder, "Die Septuagintazitate des Hebräerbriefes," in *Theologia Viatorum*, Munich, 1939, pp. 33–52; P. Padva, *Les citations de l'Ancien Testament dans l'épître aux Hébreux*, Paris, 1904; E. Hühn, *Die alttestamentlichen Citate und Reminiscenzen im Neuen Testament*, Tübingen, 1900, pp. 204 to 226.

[2] For instance in 2 Cor. 3.16 Paul reads, "but when a man turns to the Lord the veil is removed," actually citing Ex. 34.34, "but whenever Moses went in before the LORD to speak with him, he took the veil off..." J. Doeve, *Jewish Hermeneutics in the Synoptic Gospels and Acts*, Leiden, 1953, p. 98f., reasons that Paul could only have read ἐπιστρέψῃ instead of the LXX εἰσεπορεύετο by knowing that the Hebrew *bo'*, which occurs in the MT, sometimes is interchanged with *shûv* in certain textual readings as in 1 Kn. 22.27. This was sufficient reason on the grounds of Jewish exegesis for substituting the second root for the first and thus reading the meaning he wanted. See also E. Earle Ellis, *Paul's Use of the Old Testament*, Edinburgh, 1957, p. 12ff.

[3] To show the angels are certainly inferior to the Son, Heb. cites Ps. 104.4 LXX, "Who makes his angels winds, and his servants flames of fire," thus proving that such plastic creatures which can be changed suddenly into wind

Philo's arguments turn sometimes on faulty readerings of the Greek original.[4]

Philo understood all Scripture in some way as the sayings or oracles of God, although we are not at all sure how much beyond the Pentateuch his canon extended.[5] Both the utterances of God in the Decalogue and those made through an "enthused" prophet Philo regarded as oracles (*Mos.* II 67, 69).[6] Heb. similarly thinks of Scripture generally as the oracles spoken by God. God is thought of as the direct speaker in the Scripture passages cited in 1.5, 6, 7, 13; 4.3; 5.5; 6.14; 7.17, 21 (cf. 5.6); 8.5, 8–12; 10.30, 37, 38; 13.5. Scripture is referred to as "the oracles of God" in 5.12.[7] Ex. 25.40 is introduced as an oracular revelation to Moses (8.5).[8] Ps. 22.23, Is. 8.17, 18, and Ps. 40.7–9 are understood as oracles spoken by Christ (2.12f.; 10.5–7).

But it is obvious that the Biblical oracles have come through mediators as God gave them to men. The prologue says they came "through the prophets" (1.1). So when the writer first introduces Ps. 95 to his readers he says, "thus says the Holy Spirit" (3.7), and concerning Jer. 31.33f. he says, "the Holy Spirit also bears witness to us" (10.15–17); but when he cites the same psalm again he says God is speaking "by David" (4.7). Likewise he regards the priestly legislation first as revealed by the Holy Spirit (9.8), and

and fire can hardly be the addressees of Ps. 2.7 (1.6f.). But according to the MT the winds and flames are made to be the messengers and ministers of God. Similarly the writer (10.5) finds the truth that we are "sanctified through the offering of the body of Christ" in Ps. 40.7 where Christ says, "but a body thou hast prepared for me." But the MT reads literally, "but ears thou hast dug for me." σῶμα may be a corruption derived from an original reading, θελησα ΣΩΤΙΑ; see Spicq's commentary. In passages such as 10.30 and 11.17 Heb.'s readings (Dt. 32.35; Gen. 22.2) agree with the MT against all extant LXX texts. But this merely shows that the copy the writer was following coincided with the Hebrew at points where our texts do not.

[4] See C. Siegfried, *op. cit.*, p. 142.

[5] E. Goodenough, *By Light, Light*, p. 75f. Still he calls a passage in Joshua an "oracle" in *Conf.* 166.

[6] See above p. 35f.

[7] Moffatt and Riggenbach deny that the O.T. is meant by τὰ λόγια τοῦ θεοῦ. But λόγια is used in this sense elsewhere in the N.T.; cf. Rom. 3.2; Acts 7.38, although more generally in 1 Pet. 4.11. So also 1 *Clem.* 53.1; 62.3; Philo, *Legat.* 210. This fits the context as Spicq and Héring understand it.

[8] κεχρημάτισται; in Philo λόγιον and χρησμὸς are synonymous terms for divine pronouncements through a prophet, *Spec.* I 315; *Gig.* 49; *Mos.* II 188.

then as laid down by Moses (7.14). He says the Law itself was mediated by angels (2.2).[9]

We must not overlook in this connection the part angels play in prophetic inspiration according to Philo.[10] He states that the angels are "holy and divine beings, the servitors and lieutenants of the primal God whom he employs as ambassadors to announce the predictions which he wills to make to our race" (*Abr.* 115). As we have seen[11] prediction is for Philo one of the functions of prophecy. Therefore it dawned upon Sarah, says Philo, that the strangers visiting her in Gen. 18 were "prophets or angels" (*Abr.* 113). Again, the angel speaking to Balaam is made to say, "I shall guide the reins of speech, and, though you understand it not, employ your tongue for each prophetic utterance" (*Mos.* I 274). So when Heb. first says that God's revelation came through the prophets and then says that the Law came through the angels, the writer is still thinking in terms like Philo's understanding of prophecy, i.e., God's speaking through Spirit-filled men, and also by means of angels.

Philo thought that to correctly interpret inspired Scripture one must be filled with the same spirit which moved the Biblical writers and then one receives an inspired interpretation. E. F. Scott[12] expressed the view that the writer of Heb. also thought of his understanding of Scripture as having been inspired by "divine illumination."[13] But nowhere in the letter does the writer make a claim to knowledge revealed to him by inspiration. The section 5.11–6.2, however, gives us the clue to his main principle for exegeting Scripture. It stands in a parenthetic insertion (5.11–6.20) between the first mention of Christ as a priest of Melchizedek's

---

[9] ὁ δι ἀγγέλων λαληθεὶς λόγος can only mean the Law. In the letter λαλεῖν is frequently used for the communication of revelation; cf. 1.1f.; 4.8; 5.5; 7.14; 11.18; 12.25. Gal. 3.19 and Acts 7.38, 53 affirm the Jewish belief that the Law was mediated by angels at Sinai. See Strack-Billerbeck at Gal. 3.19 for evidence of this belief in Judaism. " . . . And every transgression or disobedience received a just retribution" (Heb. 2.2b) further indicates that the λόγος is the Law. λόγος is used in the sense of Law in Philo too; see *Jos.* 29; *Mig.* 105; *Mos.* II 128; *Spec.* I 273.

[10] For the following see H. Wolfson, *Philo* II, p. 44f.

[11] See above p. 32f.

[12] *Op. cit.*, p. 38.

[13] Spicq (I p. 349) takes this view too: "Seul l'Esprit divin qui a inspiré l'Écriture, peut éclairer le lecteur sur le sens christologique de cette Ecriture."

order (5.6, 10) and a *midrash* on this priestly order of Christ (7.1–28).[14] Having mentioned Christ as a priest of Melchizedek's order, before going on to his exegesis in chapter seven of Ps. 110.4, "Thou art a priest forever, after the order of Melchizedek," the writer begins his parenthetical remarks with the words, "Concerning him[15] there is much for us to say and it is difficult to interpret . . ." Then he scolds his readers for still being νήπιοι instead of τέλειοι,[16] for they need someone to go over again with them the ABC's of Biblical interpretation. But the writer is not that "someone" (τινά). For afterwards he says, leaving aside elementary things, "let us go on to maturity" (6.1). What is the maturity he is referring to? He makes it clear that it is some teaching he wishes to impart to the νήπιοι when he tells them that he is not going to go over fundamental Christian doctrine (6.1f.)—instead he is going to go on to *mature* doctrine.[17] This mature doctrine is postponed while he makes some parenetic remarks (4–12). The verses 13–20

---

[14] Spicq rightly sees this section as serving to prepare the readers for the difficult exegetical points in chapter seven.

[15] Moffatt and Westcott understand περὶ οὗ as masculine and personal.

[16] The Stoic-Pythagorean distinction (see Moffatt) of elementary teaching as milk for beginners, νήπιοι, in philosophy, and advanced doctrine as solid food for the progressed philosophers, τέλειοι, was one made by Philo (*Agr.* 9; *Cong.* 18f.; *Prob.* 160), and in the N.T. by Paul (Eph. 4.13f.). O. Michel, "Die Lehre von der christlichen Vollkommenheit nach der Anschauung des Hebräerbriefes," TSK, 1934–35, pp. 338ff., compares this passage with 1 Chron. 25.8 LXX and the contrast there between τέλειοι, meaning "teachers," and μανθάνοντες, the "learners," and suggests that the "mature" in Heb. 5.11ff. are teachers, and "infants" are pupils We must remember, however, that Philo, as well as other allegorists, sometimes used the terminology of the mystery religions to serve as technical terms of allegorical exegesis; see above pp. 42ff. He refers to those possessing the allegorical meaning of Scripture as the "initiated" (τετελέσμενοι, *Cher.* 48) who are "worthy of the holiest mystery rites" (τελεταί, *Cher.* 42), as opposed to the superstitious who never go beyond the literal meaning. In *Som.* I 164 the literalists are called ἀτέλεστοι. The *teleioi* according to Heb. 5.11–14 are the possessors of the full meaning of Scripture over against the *nepioi* who are not. So the *teleioi* in Heb. 5.14ff. may be teachers of Scripture. On the *teleioi* in mystery religion terminology, see R. Reitzenstein, *Die hellenistischen Mysterienreligionen*, p. 338f.

[17] See Héring's commentary. W. Grundmann, "Die Νήπιοι in der urchristlichen Paranese," NTS, 1959, p. 193, argues that the "faculties trained for the distinguishing between good and bad" which the *teleioi* have relate to their abilities to distinguish between the teaching which leads to salvation and false doctrine.

are introductory to and the beginning of the theme of Christ as a high priest of Melchizedek's order (20), which he then explains, having taken Ps. 110.4 (6.17) as his text. There follows (chap. 7–10) an exegesis of numerous O.T. texts, including the sacrificial institution of the old covenant, all interpreted in their relationship to Christ's work. The mature doctrine which the writer says he is going on to (6.1) therefore is a Christological exegesis of the "oracles of God" (5.12), i.e., the Old Testament. He has already admitted that such an exegesis "concerning him," i.e., Christ, is not easy to explain; it is "difficult to interpret" (5.11).

For Heb. the true meaning of the Bible is not unlocked by an inspired exegete, as in Philo's case, but rather by Christ toward whom the whole O.T. is directed (1.2). Heb. asserts it is Christ who says in Ps. 40.6–8, "Because I come, as it is written of me in the roll of the book" (10.7), and understood no doubt "the roll of the book" as the scriptures. Moses wrote "in testimony of the things to be revealed later" (τῶν λαληθησομένων, 3.5).[18] In the same way Ps. 110 and Jer. 31 are said to "bear witness" concerning Christ (7.17; 10.15). It seems likely that the writer would have said that the plan of God for salvation was a "mystery which was kept secret for long ages," but since Jesus Christ this mystery has finally come to light and "is now disclosed and through the prophetic writings is made known to all nations" (Rom. 16.25f.). Let us observe how he applies Christ as his hermeneutical guide to the Scriptures.

2: Old Testament Witnesses to Christ

We are able to reconstruct the general pattern of an exegetical argument used by the early Christians in debates with Jews over the Messianic references of the O.T. There were three standard elements in this type of argument: (1) a citation of a Scripture passage descriptive of someone, (2) a refutation of a Jewish interpretation as to whom the passage describes, (3) a demonstration that Jesus Christ is actually addressed or described by the text. This argument was used to convince Jews that Jesus was really the Christ of Israel, and we may refer to it as the "Christ-Witness

---

[18] Cf. Jn. 1.45; 5.46; Lk. 24.27, 44; Acts 26.22f.; 28.23; 2 Cor. 3.12–16.

Argument." Some illustrations of it can be seen in the N.T. In Acts 2.25–28 Peter (1) quotes David in Ps. 16.8–11, then in v. 29 (2) says that the words "For thou wilt not abandon my soul to Hades, nor let thy Holy One see corruption" could not have been describing David himself as his Jewish audience would think, for David died and was buried and thus saw corruption, so could not be the "Holy One" spoken of. Therefore the words must (3) be taken (v. 30f.) as predictive of Jesus in his resurrection, who "was not abandoned to Hades, nor did his flesh see corruption." Paul repeats the argument in 13.34–37, and in 2.33–36 Peter applies the same principles to prove that Jesus and not David is spoken of in Ps. 110.1. The Christ-Witness Argument is encountered in Mk. 12.35–37, and in the exegetical controversies of Justin, *Dialogue with Trypho the Jew*,[19] and Tertullian, *Against the Jews*.[20]

When we turn to Heb. we find that the Christ-Witness Argument is repeatedly used in the writer's Christological interpretation of the O.T. Let us consider first the exegesis of Ps. 8.5–7 (2.8f.). A Jewish interpreter would assume that the psalm is speaking of man in God's creation.[21] But Heb. argues that this is impossible, for it is obvious that all things are not placed in subjection to man as the psalm says. The words $\beta\rho\alpha\chi\acute{u}$ $\tau\iota$, which originally meant "slightly," are taken in the sense of "for a short time," and the author reasons that the phrase "Thou didst make him for a short time lower than the angels" fits Jesus during the period of his incarnation and in his humiliation perfectly; and thus he was "crowned with glory and honor," as the psalm says, by virtue of

---

[19] In 97.3f. Justin tells Trypho Ps. 22 cannot refer to David, or any other king of Israel, as Jewish exegesis would assert, because none of Israel's kings ever had his hands and feet pierced by his enemies (22.16); therefore it must refer to Christ in his crucifixion. For further examples of this argument see 33.1; 34.7; 36.2; 43; 64.5f; 83; 120.3.

[20] Tertullian insists (7) no historical king, such as Solomon, or Darius, or Alexander the Great, or Nebuchadnezzar, all of whom had limited empires, could have been addressed in Is. 45.1. He asks, who besides Christ has reigned over all the peoples of the earth, or is at the right hand of God, or whom have the Gentiles heard, that is, believed in, outside of Christ? B. P. W. Stather Hunt, *Primitive Gospel Sources*, New York, 1951, pp. 241–303, traces this argument through the following Christian dialogues with Jews: Evagrius' *Altercatio Simonis et Theophili; Jason and Papiscus; Athanasius and Zacchaeus; Timothy and Aquila*, and also the *Testimony Book of* Gregory Nyssen, and Maximus Taurinensis' *Contra Judaeos*.

[21] See Strack-Billerbeck.

his vicarious suffering.[22] The writer does not mention the significance of the term "son of man" in the psalm, but he may have thought of the title as a further indication that Jesus the Son of Man was addressed in the passage.[23]

In 1.5 the writer quotes two statements of God made to one addressed "son:" "Thou art my son, today I have begotten thee" (Ps. 2.7), and "I shall be to him a father, and he shall be to me a son" (2 Sam. 2.14). Whom would God ever address as "son" in such a way as this? A Jewish exegete could say, "Apparently God is addressing some angel in these passages, for in Gen. 6.2, 4; Ps. 29.1; 89.7; Job. 1.6; 2.1; 38.7 angels are called 'sons of God.'"[24] Heb. anticipates this interpretation, and to show that Jesus, having inherited a higher place than the angels (1.4), therefore must be addressed in these passages as "son" and not the angels, the writer cites Ps. 104.4, "Who makes his angels winds, and his servants flames of fire" (1.7).[25] Surely God would never call an ephemeral being like an angel a "son." Angels are merely "ministering spirits sent forth for service for their sakes who are about to inherit salvation" (1.14). So the "world to come" has not been subjected to them (2.5). A title like "son" would be reserved for one who had inherited a superior name than the angels, and this would be Jesus Christ (1.4).

Now angels may stand before the throne of God,[26] but Heb. asks

[22] We must not overlook, as does A. Seeberg, "Zur Auslegung von Heb. 2.5–18," NJDT, 1894, pp. 439 ff., that the present and realized fulfillment of Ps. 8 in Jesus is because he has been crowned with glory and honor in his suffering, and not because he has all things placed in subjection to him. This subjection will take place in "the world to come" (2.5). The phrase "that by the grace of God he might taste death for everyone (ὑπὲρ παντὸς)," coming as it does after the writer's interpretation of the crowning with glory and honor, is his exegesis of "thou hast placed all in subjection under his feet." Evidently he has taken τὰ πάντα here in a personal sense as in Gal. 3.22; see W. Bauer's lexicon. He finds in this statement a reference to Christ's redemption by his death of all humanity that will be under his rule in the coming age.

[23] C. H. Dodd, The Bible and the Greeks, p. 150, believes so and calls attention to the similarity between this thought and the heavenly man, or Urmensch, who in Poimandres and Philo is given the lordship over all the world and empirical man.

[24] Commenting on Gen. 6.4 Philo says that Moses sometimes "calls the angels 'sons of God'" (QG I 92).

[25] See above p. 75 n. 3.

[26] Riggenbach at 1.3 cites 1 Kn. 22.19; Is. 6.2; Zech. 3.4; Enoch 39.12; Bar. 21.6; Lk. 1.19; Rev. 7.11; 8.2.

to what angel did God ever say, "Sit at my right hand, till I make thy enemies a stool for thy feet?" (Ps. 110.1; 1.13) To sit at the throne of God in the Pseudepigraphical literature means participation in God's judgment over the world.[27] So here again Christ and not an angel must be the addressee.[28]

Here, then, are four clear instances of the Christ-Witness argument in the epistle. Since the argument is well attested in the speeches in Acts, we may quite confidently assert that Heb. is not the originator of it. But it is not whithout significance that it is more frequently encountered in Heb. than in any other N.T. document. This fact becomes especially important for us when we think of Heb.'s Alexandrian background. For in its purpose and form the Christ-Witness Argument is not unlike the reasons advanced by Philo to justify the use of allegorical exegesis. Philo asserted that if we do not apply allegorical method to the Scripture, we land in impossible absurdities.[29] Showing from time to time the absolute necessity of allegory to make sense out of certain passages of scripture, thus justifying its use at least to his own satisfaction, Philo felt at liberty on such grounds to use allegorical interpretation at will. Similarly, having established through argument that certain O.T. texts can only be understood as addressing Christ, the writer of Heb. feels about the Christological sense of Scripture as Philo did about the allegorical, namely, "if here and there, then everywhere!" So with the four cases above Heb. leaves off the Christ-Witness Argument, thinking that the Christological reference of the O.T. has been proved in enough instances and can now be taken for granted.

We have seen that the writer regards Scripture as "the oracles of God" (5.12), and understands the words of the Bible as the words of God. So when he reads the phrase in Deut. 32.43, "Let all the angels of God worship him" (1.6), he assumes (1) that God is certainly the speaker, and (2) the "him" the angels are to

---

[27] Riggenbach cites *Enoch* 51.3; 55.4; 61.8; 62.2; 69.29.

[28] If we see the depreciation of angels in Heb. 1–2 as a refutation of Jewish exegesis, there is no need to postulate angel Christologies (Michel p. 21; Windisch pp. 13, 17; Riggenbach p. 14f.) or angel veneration. (Bornkamm, *op. cit.*, col. 62f. n. 23; Moffatt p. 9; Yadin, *op. cit.*, p. 47; R. Tasker, *The Old Testament in the New Testament*, London, 1954, p. 108; T. W. Manson, "The Problem of the Epistle to the Hebrews" BJRL, 1949, p. 11f.) in the congregation.

[29] See above pp. 22–27.

worship can only be the "first-born son" of God. In 1.8f. he presupposes that Ps. 45.7f. is also an oracle of God, and therefore must be understood as addressing Christ, for only of him, the addressee of Ps. 110.1, could it be said, "Thy throne, O God, is forever and ever," since the first person of the godhead is the speaker in the psalm. The same presupposition is made for Ps. 102.26–28 (1.10f.). God can only be addressing Christ, "through whom he created the world" (1.2), when he says, "Thou, Lord, didst found the earth in the beginning . . ."

In 2.12f. the writer interprets Ps. 22.23, and Is. 8.17f. Christologically, but not as if Christ were the addressee of God's oracles as in the above passages. Now instead Christ is the speaker of these oracles in Scripture. The author likewise regards Christ as the speaker in Ps. 40.6–8 (10.5–10), and according to his own premises with good reason. He could never think that the same O.T. containing sacrificial ordinances also contains prophetic protests against their use. So he relates the protest in Ps. 40 against sacrifices which "are offered according to the law" to a later time in the *Heilsgeschichte* when by the sacrifice of Christ's body there takes place a change in the Law (7.12), whereby Christ, being the one written of "in the roll of the book," i.e., the O.T., abolishes animal sacrifices.

The writer established by his Christ-Witness Argument in 1.13 that Christ is the one spoken of in Ps. 110. He proceeds on this presupposition when he cites the fourth verse of this psalm, "The Lord has sworn and will not change his mind, 'Thou art a priest forever after the order of Melchizedek'" (5.6; 7.17, 21). Heb. strengthens his earlier contention by showing that Christ is indeed the priest here meant, for the Levitical priests (1) become priests without any oath being sworn (7.21), and (2) are not priests forever, for they are mortal and die (v. 23). But Jesus fulfills this Scripture for "he holds the priesthood permanently, because he continues forever" (v. 24).

Although the writer quotes Hab. 2.3f. (10.37f.) chiefly as a parenetic text to admonish his readers about the need to have endurance (v. 36) and not to shrink back (v. 39), by reading ὁ ἐρχόμενος instead of ἐρχόμενος ἥξει he sees in it also a promise of a speedy return of Christ.[30]

---

[30] The author's text has been altered so that instead of reading, "Coming, he will come and not linger. If anyone shrinks back, my soul takes no plea-

Many have called attention to Heb.'s seeming disregard for the context of the Scripture passages adduced as referring to Christ. If one studies the O.T. texts we have considered in their contexts, one sees that: Ps. 2.7 (1.5; 5.5) was spoken about a temporal king in Zion; Deut. 32.43 (1.6) occurs in the Song of Moses praising God; 2 Sam. 7.14 (1.5) is spoken of David's offspring, and the last part of the verse, "When he commits iniquity, I will chasten him . . . ," is incompatible with the Messiah (cf. 4.15);[31] Ps. 45.6f. (1.8f.) is said of an earthly king in his court among his concubines; Is. 8.17f. (2.13) are Isaiah's words about himself; Ps. 40 (10.5–7) is introduced as a "Psalm of David." How is it that the writer can defy the contexts of these texts and apply them all instead to Christ?

To attempt an answer to this question we must mention an hypothesis of E. Hatch[32] and F. C. Burkitt,[33] and worked out in detail by J. Rendel Harris concerning the use of "testimonies" in the early church.[34] Briefly stated, the testimony hypothesis is that one of the earliest literary documents of the Church was a collection of O.T. passages such as the volume edited in the third century by Cyprian called *Testimonia* which were proof-texts concerning Christ. The fact that certain O.T. passages are cited as witnesses to Christ by more than one N.T. writer is because the various authors derived their proof-texts from this book of testimonies in common use in the Church. C. H. Dodd has recently revised Harris' original theory,[35] dividing the N.T. corpus into

---

sure in him; but the righteous shall live by my faithfulness," in Heb. it now reads, "For yet a little while (Is. 26.20), and the coming one shall come and shall not tarry; but my righteous one shall live by faith, and if he shrinks back my soul has no pleasure in him."

[31] It is worth mentioning that this verse was interpreted messianically by the Qumran sect, see *4Q flor.* 11.

[32] *Essays in Biblical Greek*, Oxford, 1889, pp. 203 ff.

[33] *The Gospel History and its Transmission*, Edinburgh, 1907, pp. 126 ff.

[34] *Testimonies* I, II, London, 1916, 1920. The hypothesis of the testimonies was taken up by several writers after Harris, notably J. A. Findlay, "The Book of Testimonies and the Structure of the First Gospel," *The Expositor*, 1920, pp. 388–400, and "The First Gospel and the Book of Testimonies," *Amicitiae Corolla*, London, 1933, pp. 57–71; D. Plooij, *Studies in the Testimony Book*, Amsterdam, 1932; P. B. W. Stather Hunt, *op. cit.* See now the dissertation of P. Prigent, *Les testimonia dans le Christianisme primitif. L'épître de Barnabé*, Paris, 1962.

[35] *According to the Scriptures*, London, 1952.

the following blocs of independent witness to the testimonies: Paul, the Lukan, Synoptic, and Johannine writings, First Peter, and the Epistle to the Hebrews, on the presumption that when the same O.T. passage is cited by two or more separate writers, "unless there are definite reasons to the contrary, they represent to that extent a common tradition."[36] All clear allusions to a text in question as well as quotations Dodd considers as witnesses.[37] Let us examine several of the texts we have just discussed in the light of this theory.

The passage Ps. 2.7, "Thou art my beloved son, today I have begotten thee" (Heb. 1.5; 5.5), is treated as a testimony to Jesus elsewhere by Luke in Acts 13.33, and in the Synoptics in Mk. 1.11, probably in Mk. 9.7, Mt. 3.17, and the Western Text of Lk. 3.22.

Ps. 8.4–6, cited in Heb. 2.6–8 as fulfilled only in Jesus, is alluded to by Paul in 1 Cor. 15.27, Eph. 1.22, and probably Phil. 3.21. 1 Pet. 3.22 refers to it, saying Jesus has "angels, authorities, and powers subject to him" (cf. v. 6), and possibly the "honor and glory" in the hymn to the Lamb (Rev. 5.12) comes from v. 5.

Ps. 110.1 (Heb. 1.13 and afterward alluded to frequently) is quoted by Luke in Acts 2.34f., and in the Synoptics in Mk. 12.34, and phrases of it recur in Mk. 14.62, 16.19, Acts 7.55, and in Paul in Rom. 8.34, Eph. 1.20, Col. 3.1, and 1 Peter 3.22. It is a surprising fact that this text which occurs immediately prior (1.13) to Heb.'s citing of Ps. 8.5–7 (2.6f.) also is alluded to by Paul in 1 Cor. 15.25 and Eph. 1.20, 22 just before he cites a phrase from Ps. 8.7. The same phenomenon repeats itself in 1 Pet. 3.22: ". . . who has gone into heaven and is at the right hand of God, with angels, authorities, and powers subject to him ($\dot{\upsilon}\pi o\tau\alpha\gamma\acute{\epsilon}\nu\tau\omega\nu$ $\alpha\dot{\upsilon}\tau\tilde{\omega}$). This citing of or alluding to Ps. 8 immediately after Ps. 110.1 in Heb., Paul, and 1 Pet. cannot be mere coincidence. It strongly suggests the two texts were lying side by side in some document which all three writers consulted. So far as Ps. 110.4 is concerned (Heb. 6.10; 7.21), it is not cited elsewhere in the N.T., but if 110.1 stood in a list of testimonies, it is possible that the following three verses were included with it so that its citation in Heb. comes from the testimony collection.

Hab. 2.3f., cited by Heb. 10.37f. as:

---

[36] *Ibid.*, p. 30.

[37] *Ibid.*, p. 31. On the following material, see pp. 31–35, 78f., 97f.

For yet a little while, and the coming one shall come and not tarry, but my righteous one shall live by faith, and if he shrinks back, my soul has no pleasure in him.

is quoted in part by Paul in Gal. 3.11 and Rom. 1.17 as, "the righteous one shall live by faith." It is remarkable enough that both Heb. and Paul should cite this text independently of one another,[38] but it becomes all the more so when one considers that Heb.'s text has been revised in the direction of Paul's interpretation of the passage by the shifting of the possessive pronoun from "faith" to modify instead "righteous one."[39] It seems probable that both writers used a document quoting Habakkuk as a testimony to Christ in his return which emended the words, "the righteous shall live by my faithfulness," to stress instead the believer's need of faith in the latter days. Paul has quoted only the part important for his purposes.

Ps. 22.22, "I will proclaim thy name to my brethren, in the midst of the congregation I will praise thee" (Heb. 2.12), is not otherwise quoted in the N.T., but it is cited as a testimony to Christ in *Barn.* 6.16. Furthermore, in the early church the whole twenty-second psalm was a source of testimonies especially of the passion and triumph of Christ; cf. v. 6 (LXX), "why hast thou forsaken me?", Mk. 14.34; Mt. 27.46; v. 7, "they scoffed at him," Lk. 23.35; also v. 7, "they shook their heads," Mk. 15.29; v. 8, "he hoped in the Lord, let him deliver him, let him save him, for he wants him," Mt. 27.43; v. 18, "they parted my garments among themselves, and for my clothing they cast lots," Mk. 15.24; Jn. 19.24. Thus the Synoptics, John, Heb., and Barnabas all testify to a conviction that Christ is the subject in various passages of Ps. 22.

Is. 8.17f. (Heb. 2.13), like Ps. 22.23, is not otherwise cited in the N.T., but like Psalm 22 its context received a Christological interpretation in the early church. In Mt. 4.15, Is. 8.23 and 9.1 are taken as predictive of the beginning of Jesus' ministry in the vicinity of Zebulum and Naphtali. In Lk. 1.79 the phrase "to give light to those sitting in darkness and the shadow of death" (Is. 9.1) is spoken by Zechariah proleptically of Jesus. So it is con-

---

[38] That Paul is dependent on Heb. is impossible, and Heb. cites too much of the passage to be borrowing from Rom. or Gal.; see Dodd, *ibid.*, p. 51.

[39] See above p. 83 f. n. 30.

ceivable that Is. 8.17f. was retained with other passages from the same context in a list of testimonies.

The author makes use of another passage which indicates that he has used a source of testimonies when he quotes Jer. 31.31–34 (8.8–12). This text is not elsewhere quoted by N.T. writers, but it underlies certain passages in Paul. In 2 Cor. 3 Paul has the passage in mind when he speaks of being qualified as "ministers of a new covenant" (v. 6; cf. Jer. 31.31), and of "being written in our hearts" (v. 2; cf. Jer. 31.33). He mentions it by implication by referring to "the old covenant" (v. 14). In 1 Cor. 11.25, Jer. 31.31 is alluded to by the phrase "new covenant."[40]

For some time one of the standard objections to the testimony hypothesis was that no trace of Jewish collections of Scripture passages like that proposed by Harris and others had been discovered which dated from the N.T. period.[41] But now this objection falls because a text has been discovered in the Qumran find (4Q Test.) which is simply a collection of Biblical texts the sect interpreted eschatologically.[42]

It remains to compare the Christ-Witness Argument with our earlier definition of allegorical exegesis. The allegorists defined allegory as "a style speaking certain things and meaning something other than what it says."[43] To be called allegorical interpretation, an exegesis must state or presuppose that the writer of a text really meant something other than what he said. When Justin denies that Gen. 29.10 was spoken to Judah as the text says it was, saying it refers rather to Christ because only the latter can be the "expectation of the Gentiles,"[44] we have an illustration of the Christ-Witness Argument applied allegorically. One could assert that Heb. likewise has treated allegorically the passages he quotes

---

[40] Dodd, ibid., pp. 44–46.

[41] O. Michel, Paulus und seine Bibel, Gütersloh, 1929, p. 43; W. Leonard, The Authorship of the Epistle to the Hebrews, London, 1939, p. 353.

[42] J. Allegro, "Further Messianic References in Qumran Literature," JBL, 1956, p. 186, remarked when he first published it that the text belonged to the type proposed by Harris. H. Hartwig, Der Stil der jüdisch-hellenistischen Homilie, Göttingen, 1955, p. 65f. n. 12 argues that such collections were probably in use in rabbinic circles before Paul. B. P. W. Stather Hunt, op. cit., pp. 15–26, reasons that these collections of Messianic prophecies were likely in widespread use in Jewish synagogues during N.T. times.

[43] See above p. 11 n. 1.

[44] Dialogue with Trypho 120.3.

as O.T. witnesses to Christ by assigning another meaning to them than is given them by their contexts, i.e., a Christological one.[45] But to say this one would have to presuppose that the writer really read the texts in their O.T. contexts. From what we have just seen there is a strong probability that he did *not* so read them, finding them instead as isolated fragments in a book of testimonies. Except for 4.7 the writer never mentions what O.T. author or book he is quoting from. So we cannot properly say that he has interpreted allegorically any of the texts we have so far considered.

---

[45] So R. Grant, *op. cit.*, p. 55, states the O.T. is interpreted allegorically in Philo and Heb., the difference between the two lying in purpose rather than method. Philo seeks God and the soul as Heb. does Jesus, but in both cases by allegory.

CHAPTER VII

The Typological Parallel of Two Covenants

1: The Concept of Typological Exegesis

To inquire further into what was the writer's general understanding of the Scripture which he interpreted we must introduce the concept of the typological exegesis of the O.T. Today New Testament scholarship has generally settled upon a definition of the typological exegesis of the O.T. in the N.T. Typology now means the interpretation of earlier events, persons, and institutions in Biblical history which become proleptic entities, or "types," anticipating later events, persons, and institutions, which are their antitypes.[1] Thus Adam for Paul is a "type of the one to come" (Rom. 5.15), i.e., of Christ; the experiences of the Israelites in the wilderness are "types" (1 Cor. 10.6) which correspond to the experiences and temptations of the Church, having happened $\tau \upsilon \pi \iota \varkappa \tilde{\omega} \varsigma$ and having been written down "for our instruction" (v. 11).

The N.T. writers had no carefully worked out exegetical terminology,[2] and the word "type" is not mentioned as a technical term of N.T. hermeneutics aside from these passages. But typology as we have defined it above can be seen throughout the N.T. 1 Pet.

---

[1] G.W.H. Lampe, and K.J. Woolecombe, *Essays on Typology*, London, 1957, pp. 27–31; 59; R. Bultmann, "Ursprung und Sinn der Typologie als hermeneutische Methode," TL, 1950, col. 206; H. Wolff, "The Hermeneutics of the Old Testament," *Interpretation*, 1961, pp. 457 ff.; L. Goppelt, *Typos: Die typologische Deutung des Alten Testaments im Neuen*, Gütersloh, 1939, p. 244; W. Eichrodt, "Ist die typologische Exegese sachgemässe Exegese?", TL, 1956, col. 641–654; C. Spicq, commentary I, p. 346. Both "type" ($\tau \acute{\upsilon} \pi o \varsigma$, lit., "impression") and "antitype" ($\dot{\alpha} \nu \tau \acute{\iota} \tau \upsilon \pi o \varsigma$) are ambiguous in their usages, and both can mean "copy'," or "pattern;" cf. Bauer's lexicon, *ad verba*. The contrast "type-antitype" is a refined one as applied in this definition of typology.

[2] W. Eichrodt, *op. cit.*, p. 211.

3.20f. seems to use the word "antitype" in such a technical sense in describing the typology of the Flood to Christian baptism: "... in the days of Noah ... eight persons were saved through water. And now baptism, as an antitype of the flood ($\dot{a}\nu\tau\dot{i}\tau\upsilon\pi\sigma\nu$), saves you."[3] The destruction of the Flood, and the burning of Sodom are types of the eschatological judgment (Lk. 17.26–32; Mt. 24.37–39). The tribulations of Ex. 7–10 are types for the woes of the end-time (Rev. 16). As we shall see later Moses is frequently portrayed in the N.T. as a type of Christ. His lifting up the serpent in the wilderness is a type of the Son of Man's crucifixion (Jn. 3.14). Jonah's remaining in the belly of the whale three days and three nights is a type, i.e., "sign," of the three-day burial of the Son of Man (Mt. 12.38–40).

Writers frequently differentiate typology from allegory in this way:

> While for typology the historical importance of the text being interpreted forms the essential presupposition of its use, for allegory on the other hand it is indifferent, or even offensive, and must be pushed aside in order to liberate the "spiritual" meaning lying behind it.[4]

This distinction would need to be qualified somewhat to differentiate from typology the apocalyptic allegorization of Biblical history making it refer to contemporary history. We should add that typology does not assert, as allegory does, that the text means something other ($\check{a}\lambda\lambda\sigma\varsigma$) than what it says. Typology presumes nothing more than that an event, person, or institution occurring at one point in Biblical history will find a counterpart at a later point in history. It does not dissolve the historical character of the event, person, or institution to find another meaning behind it—not even a futuristic one, as is done, for instance, in the Qumran *Habakkuk Commentary*. It is applying to Scripture the same

---

[3] It is not certain whether "antitype" in this sentence has a different meaning than in Heb. 9.24 or not. If B. Reicke, *The Disobedient Spirits and Christian Baptism*, Lund, 1946, pp. 144ff., is right that the phrase ὃ καὶ ὑμᾶς ἀντίτυπον νῦν σῴξει βάπτισμα should be translated "which 'antitypical' baptism now saves you," then the clause is speaking of Noah's diluvial baptism which is a type of Christian baptism, just as the sanctuary made with hands (Heb. 9.24) is an "antitype" typifying the real one in heaven. In this usage antitype would correspond to type in our earlier definition. But see E. Selwyn, *The First Epistle of St. Peter*, London, 1946, p. 298f; Per Lundberg, *La typologie baptismale dans l'ancienne Eglise*, Uppsala, 1942, p. 110f.

[4] W. Eichrodt, *op. cit.*, col. 643.

principle of comparison which saw in Drake's battle with the Spanish Armada an anticipation of Britain's campaign with Germany in the '40's.[5]

It should not be surprising that typological exegesis is totally absent from Philo's writings, and the word τύπος does not appear as a technical exegetical term there as it does in the N.T. and Apostolic Fathers.[6] As we shall see, this exegetical concept is basic to Heb.'s interpretation of the O.T., and differs radically from Philo's method in this important respect.

Nevertheless the typology of Heb. is of a peculiar kind, and it seems necessary to carry our definition still further to accurately describe it. When Heb. parallels the once a year entrance of the high priest into the second tent with Christ's ascension into the heavenly tabernacle (9.6–12), we have an example of an interpretation of an event in the O.T. which becomes a type anticipating a later event which is its antitype. But in Heb. the typology of events, persons, and institutions is drawn because there is first a typological parallelism between the old and the new covenants.

---

[5] Lampe-Woolcombe, *op. cit.*, p. 20. H. Wolfson, *The Philosophy of the Church Fathers* I, p. 27, cites as illustrative of a typological reading of the Bible *Sotah* 34a, according to which the events that happened to the patriarchs are a sign *(siman)* of what is to happen to their offspring.

[6] H. de Lubac, "'Typologie' et 'allegorisme,'" *Recherches 1e Science Religieuse*, 1947, p. 184. In *Opif.* 157 allegorizing the Genesis narration of creation and the Fall, Philo says, "Now these are no mythical fictions, such as poets and sophists delight in, ἀλλὰ δείγματα τύπων ἐπ' ἀλληγορίαν παρακαλοῦντα κατὰ τὰς δι' ὑπονοιῶν ἀποδόσεις. The key term is not τύπος, but δεῖγμα, which has a history in Greek exegesis and means in Philo a specimen for allegorical study; see below, p.96f. τύπος probably denotes here "principle," as in Plato, *Rep.* 379A, 380C; see J. Tate, "Plato and Allegorical Interpretation," *CQ*, 1927, p. 145; also Liddell-Scott, *ad verb.*

In the Church Fathers the term τύπος applied to exegesis has a varied use. In *Dial. with Trypho* 134 Justin uses the word in the same sense as we have defined typological exegesis in the N.T., saying that the marriages of Jacob were types of that which Christ was to accomplish, and that Moses and Joshua anticipated Christ in 91.3 and 11.2. But in 90.2 he uses "type" as an equivalent for allegory. Also in *Barn.* 7.10f., and 12.6, 10 "type" is employed in the sense of typological exegesis; but in 8.1f. it is meant allegorically, for of the type in Num. 19 he says, "the calf is Jesus." The last passage simply identifies the old and the new, a presupposition for all Christian allegorizing of the O.T. (cf. H. Wolff, *op. cit.*, 464). This shows that we must not expect to find in connection with the patristic use of τύπος always the same concept we have defined for N.T. typological exegesis.

Basic to Heb.'s understanding of scripture is *Heilsgeschichte*. As if it were a presupposition to everything following, in the prologue the writer takes note that in the past God has repeatedly spoken to Israel by the prophets (1.1), but at the mid-point of time[7] he has acted decisively for salvation by sending his Son who through his death has made it possible for those eagerly awaiting Christ's return (9.28) to be saved (1.2f.; 9.28). He speaks of God leading "the first-born into the world" at this mid-point in history (1.6).[8] This period when Christ offered a single sacrifice for sins "for all time" (10.12; 14), and "once for all" (εφάπαξ 7.27; 9.12; 10.10; cf. ἅπαξ 9.26, 28) was not simply a period in which a pre-existent heavenly man, "who for a little while was made lower than the angels" (2.9), entered the world coming from the heavenly spheres in his humiliation, and ascended again into the heavens in his exhaltation taking the believers with him. It was also "the days of his flesh" which was a time of real and earthly trial and learning for the Lord who finally "became a source of eternal salvation to all who obey him" (5.9). During these days this salvation "was proclaimed at first by the Lord," and was confirmed by human and divine witness together (2.3f.).

This mid-point in history, which the O.T. looks forward to and the writer reflects back upon, has broken the *Heilsgeschichte* into two halves. By saying, "at the end of these days God spoke to us by a son" (1.2), he means that in the revelation through the Son the pre-eschatological period has come to an end and a new period in *Heilsgeschichte* has begun.[9] It is also possible that H. L.

---

[7] See the phrase "at the end of these days" (1.2) below on this page.

[8] ὅταν δὲ πάλιν εἰσαγαγῃ κ. τ. λ. must be translated "and again he says when he leads the first-born into the world," rather than "and when he leads the first-born into the world again," i.e., at the second coming. Moffatt notes the idiomatic reference of εἰσάγειν to a birth. The introduction to Ps. 40.7–9 applied to Christ's atoning death reads similarly: "Therefore entering into the world (Christ) says . . . " (10.5), and this favors taking 1.6 as referring to Christ's first entry into the world also.

[9] G. Kittel, TWNT II, p. 695, compares this statement in 1.2 with 1 Pet. 1.20 according to which Christ "was manifest ἐπ' ἐσχάτου τῶν χρόνων for the uniquely N.T. idea the latter days have broken in with Jesus Christ, and a new stage in the *Heilsgeschichte* has come. Phrases like ἡ ἐσχάτη ἡμέρα (Jn. 6.39, 44, 54; 11.24; 12.48; cf. Mt. 5.26; Lk. 12.59; 1 Cor. 15.26, 52; Rev. 15.1; 21.9; Acts 2.17; 2 Tim. 3.1) are repeatedly used in the N.T. to refer to the last day of the resurrection and judgment. ἐπ' ἐσχάτου τῶν ἡμερῶν is the

MacNeill is right that when the writer says at the end of 1.2 that through the Son God "made τοὺς αἰῶνας," he is thinking not of the world (cf. 11.3; 9.26), but the two ages, or economies, between which Christ is the mid-point.[10] Phrases such as "the time of the new order" (9.10) and "the present period" (9.9) demarcate this age from the former one.

In dividing the *Heilsgeschichte* into two halves Christ also divided it into an old (8.9) and a new covenant (8.8, 13; 9.15; 12.24), into a first (8.7, 13; 9.1) which is succeeded by a second (8.7, 13). Heb. was called by W. Wrede a study concerning "the relationship of the old and the new covenants."[11] In this the writer's chief task is to compare the features of the new covenant which are paralleled in the old. Thus, the first had regulations for worship (9.1) which anticipated Christ's priestly work (9.11–10.25), and a sanctuary which paralleled the "greater and more perfect tabernacle" in heaven into which Christ later ascended (9.11, 24). The members of the new covenant are εὐηγγελισμένοι just as the members of the old (4.2); the new covenant has been νενομοθέτηται (8.6) just as the old (7.11).[12] In both covenants there is no forgiveness of sins without the shedding of blood (9.22). The first covenant was inaugurated in blood (9.18), and in like manner Christ set up the new covenant through his own blood (9.12).

The parallelism of the two covenants is basic to the typology of Heb., and Ellis[13] and Wolff[14] see it underlying other typological passages in the N.T. According to Heb. nothing in the new covenant has arisen which has not its counterpart in the old; but the new is not simply a repetition of the old.[15] Just as in Rom.

LXX translation of *bᵉʾhrîth hāyyamîm* (Num. 24.14; Jer. 23.20; Dan. 10.14), and corresponds to the Targumic *bᵉsôph yômᵃyyäʾ*, i.e., the final days and times of the Messiah; see Strack-Billerbeck. Spicq notes τούτων puts the Messianic age into the present generation.

[10] *The Christology of the Epistle to the Hebrews*, Chicago, 1914, p. 17; similarly J. Bonsirven, *St. Paul, Épître aux Hébreux*, Paris, 1943, p. 171f.; J. Van der Ploeg, "L'exégèse de l'Ancien Testament dans l'épître aux Hébreux," RB, 1947, p. 189.

[11] *Das literarische Rätsel des Hebräerbriefes*, Göttingen, 1906, p. 66.

[12] E. Lohmeyer, *Diatheke. Ein Beitrag zur Erklärung des neutestamentlichen Begriffes*, Leipzig, 1913, p. 144.

[13] *Op. cit.*, p. 130f. on Gal. 4.22ff., 1 Cor. 5.7, 10.2ff., and numerous other passages.

[14] *Op. cit.*, p. 454ff.

[15] O. Michel, commentary, p. 47.

5.14ff. Christ is not merely a repetition of his type, Adam, but differs from him as well as resembling him, and in 2 Cor. 3.7ff. the splendor of the new dispensation is greater than that revealed to Moses, so for Heb. the new covenant, typified in the old, is better and more perfect than the former one (7.22; 8.6; 9.11).[16]

Thus the anticipations of the old covenant of the new are *parabolic*. Of the tabernacle sacrifices the writer says:

> After these things were thus established, the priests performing their services of worship enter the first tent continually. But the high priest alone goes into the second tent once a year. This is done not without blood which he offers for himself and for the sins committed in ignorance by the people. By this the Holy Spirit indicates that the way into the sanctuary is not yet opened as long as the first tent (σκηνή) is still standing, ἥτις παραβολὴ εἰς τὸν καιρὸν ἐνεστηκότα according to which gifts and sacrifices are offered which are unable to perfect the worshipper's conscience. They are only fleshly regulations on food, drink, and various ablutions, imposed until the time of the new order. (9.6–10)

By stating that the order of the cult indicates that the "way into the sanctuary is *not yet* opened," and that the cultic regulations were imposed "*until* the time of the new order," one would at first expect the writer to say that the first tent is parabolic of the *former* time and not of the *present*. When he states that the sanctuary is parabolic of the present time, indicating that the way into it is not yet opened, he seems to contradict 10.20 which says the way is now open. What, then, does he mean saying that the first tent is a parable of the present time?

The term "parable" in Greek is a rather general one, and although A. Jülicher wanted to distinguish sharply between a parable and an allegory,[17] this is not always possible, for the word has a history as a technical term in both pre-Christian and Christian allegorical exegesis.[18] Just as "type" has a varied and wide usage

---

[16] E. Lohmeyer, *op. cit.*, p. 146; W. Eichrodt, *op. cit.*, p. 206. This feature is overlooked by Bultmann, *op. cit.*, p. 206, stating that typology presupposes a cyclical repetition view of history.

[17] *Die Gleichnisreden Jesu*[2] I, Leipzig, 1899, p. 58f.; so W. Gunkel, "Allegorie," in RGG[2] II, 219f.; F. Hauck, TWNT V, p. 742.

[18] R. Grant, *op. cit.*, p. 133f. We should note that "parable" is not an exegetical term in Philo. H. Wolfson, *The Philosophy of the Church Fathers* I, pp. 31–41, tries to show that "parable" as well as "type" in the N.T. were technical words of exegesis "borrowed from Philo's vocabulary" (p. 41). But he is only able to cite *Opif.* 157 for "type," which we discussed above

and its context finally determines its meaning, so it is in the case of "parable."[19]

If in Heb. 9.9 the writer had said that the first tent is a parable for the former time before Christ's priestly work, we would have the kind of allegorization encountered in Gal. 4.22ff. The first tent would have stood for the old covenant, and the once a year entrance of the high priest into the second could have represented Christ's ascending into the holy of holies in heaven as the priest of the new covenant in the same way as in Paul's allegory the two wives of Abraham represent the two covenants. In v. 8 Heb. offers no pneumatic exegesis, stating the simple fact that so long as worship was taking place in the outer tent the way to the sanctuary, either earthly or heavenly, was not yet revealed. But v. 9 introduces a new thought, suddenly speaking about the present time instead of the past as in v. 8, saying that the first tent is parabolic for the present age. The writer means the same situation which existed before the way into the sanctuary was revealed from at least one perspective also obtains today. Since for the Christians the way into the sanctuary is already open (10.19f.), the parable of the first tent can only be related to the Jews who still stand in the pre-Messianic posture occupied by the people of God when the way into the sanctuary had not yet been revealed. In vv. 9 and 10 the writer states how the situation stands at present in Judaism. According to the parable ($\varkappa\alpha\vartheta'\ \mathring{\eta}\nu$) which the worship in the first tent offers concerning the Jews today, regulations on gifts, food, drink, offerings, and ablutions are still being offered which were at best external in former days and were intended only up to the "time of the new order." The parable, then, for the present time is one in which under the old covenant (9.1) worship in the first tent outside the sanctuary is a type for the present-day situation of Judaism. During these days of the new covenant Judaism is still outside the sanctuary. In the verses following Heb. undertakes a similar comparison which we will take up later[20] between the work of the high priest under the old covenant and Christ's work under the new.

----

p. 91 n. 6. For "parable" he notes *Conf.* 99 where the term means "allegory." But Leisegang's *Indices* show no other occurrences of it, so "parable" could not have been a part of Philo's exegetical terminology.

[19] In *Herm. Similitudes* II 2 parable and type are synonyms.

[20] See below p. 119ff.

"Parable" is used once more in Heb. 11.19 where Abraham, about to offer Isaac, "considered that God was able to raise men even from the dead; hence $\grave{\varepsilon}\nu\ \pi\alpha\varrho\alpha\beta o\lambda\tilde{\eta}$ he did receive him back." Very early Christians saw in the offering of Isaac a type of Christ,[21] and although the writer does not mention Christ in this context there are the following indications that $\grave{\varepsilon}\nu\ \pi\alpha\varrho\alpha\beta o\lambda\tilde{\eta}$ means, "in typical parallel to Christ":[22] (1) Heb. says Abraham believed God was able to raise Isaac from the dead even though Gen. 22 does not say this. This seems to connect Abraham's receiving Isaac back parabolically for the writer with Christ's resurrection. (2) The death of Isaac was to be a sacrificial offering, just as Christ's death is a sacrifice in 5.3, 9.28, 10.12, *et passim*. (3) Abraham's offering of his $\mu o\nu o\gamma\varepsilon\nu\grave{\eta}\varsigma$ (11.17) corresponds to God's giving his only son whom the writer calls the $\pi\varrho\omega\tau\acute{o}\tau o\varkappa o\varsigma$ (1.6).

We see in these instances, then, the comparison of parallels in the two covenants expressed by the term "parable."

Likewise the writer says that the typical relationship between features in both covenants is *digmatic*. Jude 7 says that Sodom and Gomorrah in their destruction "are set forth as a $\delta\varepsilon\tilde{\iota}\gamma\mu\alpha$, undergoing a punishment of eternal fire." 2 Pet. 2.6 in literary dependence upon this passage replaces $\delta\varepsilon\tilde{\iota}\gamma\mu\alpha$ with the synonym $\acute{\upsilon}\pi\acute{o}\delta\varepsilon\iota\gamma\mu\alpha$ —God set an example "for those who were to act ungodly ($\mu\varepsilon\lambda\lambda\acute{o}\nu\tau\omega\nu$ $\grave{\alpha}\sigma\varepsilon\beta\varepsilon\tilde{\iota}\nu$)." The basic meaning of these two words is "example" (cf. Jn. 13.15; Jam. 5.10), being synonymous also with $\pi\alpha\varrho\acute{a}\delta\varepsilon\iota\gamma\mu\alpha$. But $\delta\varepsilon\tilde{\iota}\gamma\mu\alpha$ and $\acute{\upsilon}\pi\acute{o}\delta\varepsilon\iota\gamma\mu\alpha$ were also technical words of allegory, used as such by Philo.[23] In Philo the terms when used allegorically meant subjects for allegorical interpretation, such as Adam, Eve, and the serpent (*Opif.* 157), the laying of one's hands on the head

---

[21] *Barn.* 7.3. E. Goodenough, *Jewish Symbols in the Greco-Roman Period* IV, New York, 1954, p. 179 ff., thinks it possible that the Christian comparison of the death of Christ with Isaac's sacrifice goes back to a Jewish tradition which among other things likened the wood for Isaac's offering to the cross carried by a criminal. Assembling the evidence for this view, he proposes that Heb. has cut short the tradition still reflected in this passage. Such a Jewish tradition on Isaac is not shown in Philo's extant writings. But Goodenough (p. 191) further speculates that the reason Philo's *On Isaac* was lost is because Christians suppressed it, for what Philo said about Isaac they wanted to be said only of Christ.

[22] Several Greek commentators understood the passage to be intending Isaac as a type of Christ; see Spicq.

[23] See above p. 20.

of a sacrificial victim (*Spec.* I 202), the members of animals sacrificed (*Sac.* 139). The verb ὑποδείκνυμι is used to mean "to show an allegorical truth" in *Mut.* 69.

Having cited Ps. 95.7–11, and commenting on the apostasy of the Israelites in the wilderness, Heb. 4.11 says, "Let us therefore strive to enter into that rest, lest anyone fall by the same ὑπόδειγμα of disobedience. ὑπόδειγμα is here applied to an O.T. incident which becomes a parenetic warning for the new Christian community, just as in Jude 7, and 2 Pet. 2.6 above, and 1 *Clem.* 5.1. As God punished offenders in these ways in the past, so he will punish evil-doers in the future. In other words, Heb. 4.11 has taken a term used in Philo for subjects of allegorical study in Scripture and applied it to a typal passage in the O.T., parenetically showing its significance for the people of the new covenant. The other two instances of ὑπόδειγμα, 8.5 and 9.23, are more complex in their meanings, and we must defer discussing them for the moment.[24]

It is interesting to contrast the concept of Scripture just described with the allegorical-literal, two-layer theory in Philo. In Heb.'s view there are not two meanings lying within the text. The writer never exposits a literal followed by a "deeper" sense. Instead he is comparing persons, events, and institutions manifested in the first covenant with their respective parallels in the new covenant. His presupposition is that the former features will always find some kind of counterparts in the second covenant.

2: The Understanding of the Law

We have shown that Philo's claim that the Torah mirrored the eternal Law of Nature saved it from Hellenism's relativizing of the written laws of other nations and states whose contradictory demands mutually cancel each other's claim to absoluteness. By conforming to the Law of Nature the Torah answered the first requirement of law according to Hellenism. Philo argued that the Law answered the second Hellenistic requirement of law, namely, that the true Law be written in the souls of those living by it because in effect the O.T. legislation was merely copied from the lives of the patriarchs as νόμοι ἔμψυχσι who embody the Law of

---

[24] See below p. 110f.

Nature. But in taking over the current philosophical understanding of Law, Philo automatically placed the Torah under the same scrutiny that all other laws and constitutions underwent. Thus, if someone had demonstrated against Philo's assertion that the Torah in fact did not meet these two qualifications, then the Torah would have to be given up, for Philo's apology for the Law at the same time robbed it of any unique authority of its own.[25]

Heb. contains a sharp criticism of the Law of Moses. The writer notices that the Law of Moses was a moral one, and that transgressions against it were punished as such (2.2; 10.28). For him the term Law means the whole O.T. Law in contrast to the different commandments of it (7.5; 9.19). It is essentially a religious constitution in which the priesthood with its sacrificial duties forms the center (7.11, 12, 28; 8.4; 9.22). One objection Heb. brings against this religious constitution is that it did not bring the believers to perfection (7.11, 19; 10.1). What is meant by "perfection" we shall take up later.[26]

A further objection against the Law, either aimed directly at the Philonic doctrine that the Torah is eternal because it embodies the unchanging and eternal Law of Nature, or at any rate against the general Jewish doctrine of the eternity of the Torah,[27] is that the Law was limited to a specific period in the past, and therefore, in contrast to the new covenant of salvation, is not eternal. The writer's argument takes up O.T. proof-texts to show that the Law was never intended to last eternally, that it was only for the period up to "the time of the new order" (9.10). First he cites Ps. 110.4, "Thou art a priest forever after the order of Melchizedek" (5.6), applied to Jesus. When this passage appoints another priest and introduces a change, shifting the priesthood from the order of Aaron to that of Melchizedek (7.11), it follows "when there is a change in the priesthood, there must be a change of Law" (7.12),

---

[25] See above pp. 44–48.

[26] See below pp. 112 ff.

[27] It probably never occurred to Pharisaic and apocalyptic Judaism to press the Hellenistic Law of Nature into service in order to show the Torah was eternal, but it was often said by late-Judaism that the Torah was created before the world (*Gen. R.* I 4), engraven on heavenly tablets (*The Book of Noah* 106.19; *Test. Levi* 5.4; *Jub.* 15.25; 30.9; 33.10, *et passim*), and from time to time revealed to the patriarchs, and finally revealed to Moses by the angels of the presence (*Jub.* 1.26–29), who simply wrote down what was already on the heavenly tablets (*Jub.* 23.32).

and a change in the Law amounts to its termination. This the writer makes clear by citing another proof-text, Ps. 40.7–9, put in Jesus' mouth:

> Thou hast not desired sacrifices and offerings, but a body thou hast prepared for me;
> thou hast not taken pleasure in burnt offerings for sins.
> Then I said, " . . . lo! I come, to do thy will, O God. (10.5–7)

The writer explains that sacrifices, offerings, and burnt offerings are items offered in accordance with the Law. When Christ says he is coming to do God's will, "He abolishes the first (the Law) in order to establish the second (God's will)," since God has no desire for the Torah's sacrifices (10.8f.).

A third proof-text used for the same end is Jer. 31.31–34, the passage concerning the new covenant (8.8–12). Had the writer been asked to differentiate between the old covenant and the Law, he probably would not have drawn much if any distinction between the two. At certain passages the Law and the new covenant are juxtaposed as if they were the old and the new covenants. Just as one who rejected the Law of Moses was punished, so even greater punishment will be inflicted upon anyone who spurns Christ, the Spirit of grace, "and the blood of the covenant . . . in which he was hallowed" (10.28f.). The writer says the new covenant of which Jesus is mediator "νενομοθέτηται upon better promises" (8.6). So he thought of a certain parallel between the giving of the Law[28] and the establishing of the new covenant. Except that it would have disturbed his argument concerning the covenant, he could just as well have said "Law" instead of "covenant" in 9.15: ". . . those who are called may receive the promised eternal inheritance, since a death has occurred which redeems them from the transgressions[29] under the first covenant" (9.15). He calls the tables of the Law the "tablets of the covenant" (9.4). So the "first covenant," in connection with the Jeremiah citation (8.7, 13), is synonymous with the Law which God implies is "becoming obsolete and growing old, near to destruction."

As the writer found in Jer. 31.31–34 a proof that the Law was not eternal, he also found there the words, "This is the covenant that I will make with the house of Israel after those days, says the

---

[28] Cf. the same verb in 7.11.
[29] For παράβασις applied to infractions of the Law, cf. 2.2.

Lord: I will put my laws into their minds and write them on their hearts" (8.10). This he quotes again at 10.16, striking at another claim for the Law made by Philo when he stated it was first engraved inwardly on the patriarchs' souls before being written by Moses. Heb. takes up the same Hellenistic minimizing of written law which prompted Philo to show that the Law is in fact based on νόμοι ἔμψυχοι. Heb. notes that according to Jer. 31.33 the first covenant, the Law, was not written inwardly, that is, engraved on the hearts or souls of those following it—this is done only in the new covenant. The laws of the old covenant, far from being written on the minds and hearts of the believers, are "regulations of the flesh" (9.10). So also the priest of the new covenant, Jesus, did not become a priest like the priest of the old covenant who took office "according to the Law of a fleshly commandment" (7.16).[30]

But as opposed to the Law which was neither inscribed inwardly nor eternal, the new covenant is both. Jesus, unlike the Law's priests who live and die, come and go (7.8, 23), "remains a priest forever" (6.20; 7.3, 24, 28) of an eternal covenant (13.20). He has become a priest "because of the power of an *indestructible* life" (7.16); he "lives *always* to make intercession" (7.25; cf. v. 8). He has the priesthood "unchangeably" and therefore is "*always* able to save . . ." (7.24f.).[31] He is "the same yesterday, today, and forever" (13.8). He has obtained an "eternal redemption" (9.12) "through the eternal Spirit" (9.14) so that the elect may receive an "eternal inheritance" (9.15). This he did "once for all" (7.27; 10.10).

It is a further idea of Heb. that what the Law could apply only externally to the worshipper, in the new covenant has become an

---

[30] I am sure that G. Milligan, *The Theology of the Epistle to the Hebrews*, Edinburgh, 1899, p. 120, is right that σάρκινος here has no idea of moral blame attached to it like in Rom. 7.14 and σαρκικὸς has elsewhere in the N.T. It designates the lack of spiritual, heavenly, and eternal power. Although the distinction between the adjective endings ιχὸς and ινος is not always present in Hellenistic Greek, Westcott's coining the word "fleshen" to render σάρκινος is useful here. In the 2nd cent. the term was used for by-products of animals, such as leather rope. See J. Moulton, G. Milligan, *The Vocabulary of the Greek Testament*, London, 1928, *ad verb.* W. Gutbrod, TWNT IV, p. 1071, paraphrases the sense, "nach dem in fleischlichem Gebot bestehenden Gesetz."

[31] So εἰς τὸ παντελὲς is taken by the Vulgate, Windisch, and Strathmann.

inward and spiritual quality, so that the Law is put into the mind and written on the heart (8.10; 10.16). Philo's contention was that the rites of the Law cleansed a man both in soul and body:

> The law would have such a person pure in body and soul, the soul purged of its passions and distempers and infirmities and every viciousness of word and deed, the body of the defilements which commonly beset it. For each it devised the purification which befitted it. For the soul it used the animals which the worshipper is providing for sacrifice, for the body sprinklings and ablutions . . . (*Spec.* I 257f.).

In the words following, Philo argues in the way we have earlier noted[32] that the Law's rituals connected with the sacrifice of animals have symbolic references to the reformation of the soul's conduct, and so the Law cleansed the soul. But in trying to show the externalism of the whole Law, Heb. reiterates the Hellenistic critique against all sacrificial rites which had prompted Jews like Philo and Aristeas to justify them with elaborate allegorizations on their meanings for the soul and mind. Heb. almost seems to have the above passage of Philo in mind when he contradicts it saying:

> For if the sprinkling of defiled persons with the blood of goats and bulls and with the ashes of a heifer sanctifies for the purification of the flesh, how much more shall the blood of Christ, who through the eternal spirit offered himself without blemish to God, purify your conscience from dead works to serve the living God (9.13f.).

The writer moves all the O.T. sacrificial and purification rites[33] into the category of purifying the body or flesh,[34] a category which for Philo applied merely to the Law's ablutions and sprinklings for purification, and says only Christ's blood can purify the

---

[32] See above pp. 50ff.

[33] The "goats and bulls" refer, of course, to the offerings of Lev. 16, a chapter the writer refers to throughout his discussion of O.T. sacrifices. But the ashes of the heifer are an allusion to the rites of purification from defilement of touching dead bodies; cf. Num. 19.9f. Riggenbach has shown the contrasting thought: Just as contact with a *corpse* under the old covenant is defiling and ashes are needed to purify one, so Christ in the new covenant by his purification cleanses us from *dead* works.

[34] I do not think there is any significance to Philo's speaking of the purification of the *body* and Heb. speaking of the *flesh*. Philo's body-soul dualism sometimes is spoken of as a flesh-soul dualism; cf. *Gig.* 31, "souls that are free from flesh and body . . . " Philo could just as easily have spoken of a flesh-soul contrast in *Spec.* I 257f.

conscience, a function Philo would have claimed for animal sacrifices which purify the soul. Here and in other passages in the epistle the writer means by conscience that awareness within the understanding which is disturbed and pained whenever man commits moral offences.[35] The charge laid against the Law is that its ritualism merely touches the flesh and never rids one of the bad conscience within one which frustrates the worship of God. But Christ has purified the conscience of the worshipper by taking away sins (9.15, 26, 28a; 10.12) so that for him there is no longer a reminder of past sins (10.3) to pain him.

The same contrast Law-flesh, and new covenant-pure conscience lies behind other passages. The gifts and offerings of the Law are unable to perfect the worshipper so far as his conscience is concerned (9.9). If this were not so, the writer asks, "would not the

---

[35] C. A. Pierce, *Conscience in the New Testament*, London, 1955, pointing out that συνείδησις and its cognates are never defined in the N.T., has attempted to come to an understanding of the concept primarily through its popular use in Hellenistic literature, the papyri, and inscriptions, but also through its classical instances. He shows that there are two basic categories, a non-moral, semi-technical context in which αὐτῷ συνειδέναι means "I am conscious of . . . within myself," and a moral use in which the content of this knowing is the moral significance of the person's behaviour (p. 21). Pierce finds no instances of the first type in the N.T. (61), although in 1 Pet. 2.19 the noun means "awareness" (108). He further subdivides the moral usages of the term which were its predominant popular applications (22ff.). "The fundamental connotation of the συνείδησις group of words is that man is by nature so constituted that, if he oversteps the moral limits of his nature he will normally feel pain—the pain called συνείδησις" (50). Therefore the term "good conscience" (cf. Heb. 13.18) means simply the absence of conscience's pains (39; 51), which is confirmed by the word's N.T. usages (94ff.) "Conscience—the judge" makes one aware of his evil past acts so that the term is almost always connected with shame (54). In the LXX the concept appears only in the Wisdom Literature (Job. 27.6; *Wisd.* 17.11). Philo witnesses to its usual meaning: The reasonable mind "dwelling in the soul of each of us . . . convicts us from within" using the reins of the conscience (*Det.* 23); we are "convicted by conscience of our own unrighteous acts" (*Spec.* II 49; cf. "conscience of certain sins," *Virt.* 124 and Heb. 10.2). Pierce states the N.T. writers take up this popular concept, but for them conscience alone is never enough. He paraphrases 1 Cor. 4.4, "This conscience . . . that you keep throwing in my face—I grant you that it has its uses. It's no good, however, telling me your conscience is clear. Mine is clear too but that is not enough —'yet am I not hereby justified'" (65). Man must follow conscience, but his conscience is not his only guide because faith (109f.) and the Holy Spirit (Rom. 9.1, p. 84) must inform it.

things being offered have stopped, on account of the worshippers being cleansed once and no longer having a conscience of sins?" (10.2) It is reported that Aaron and his sons were washed (Ex. 29.4, λούσεις; Lev. 8.6, ἔλουσεν) with water and sprinkled (Ex. 29.21, ῥανεῖς; Lev. 8.30, προσέρρανεν) with the blood of the altar before serving God at the tent of meeting. Having paralleled the blood sprinklings of the Law with Christ's blood (9.13f.; cf. 12.24; 13.20), the writer declares that the Christians may draw near to God because their hearts are sprinkled (ῥεραντίσμένοι) and made clean from an evil conscience, and their bodies are washed (λελουσμένοι) with pure water (10.22). The water here mentioned must refer to baptism (cf. 6.2) whose types in the old covenant were the ablutions of the priests.[36] In 1 Pet. 3.21 the type of baptism is the flood at the time of Noah. The latter passage also differs from Heb. 10.22, taking baptism as a symbol for the petition to God for a *good conscience*. For Heb. baptism is the washing of the body corresponding to the Law's ritual provisions for the same and contains no reference in it to the cleansing of the conscience. Contrary to Philo's assertion, for Heb. the soul or heart is not cleansed by the sprinkling of animal blood, but by Christ's, so that the writer can speak of the Christians' "being sprinkled," followed by the accusative, "with respect to the hearts from an evil conscience."

The idea of the conscience's purification, never affected by the Law, but achieved by Christ, was most important for the writer in his debate with Judaism. He had to overrule Jewish apologists like Philo who were trying to establish the precepts of the Torah inwardly by complicated allegorization to make its contents apply to the life of the soul. Heb. wants to show that such spiritual references are simply not in the Law at all, for it dealt only with external things, and it is only in the new covenant, promised through Jeremiah, which is written on the heart and mind of the worshipper (8.10; 10.16), now because of the cleansing of the conscience due to Christ's work.

But it is not as if the Law had no relation to the new covenant. Before stating that the Law's sacrifices never could make the worshippers perfect, the writer says: "For the Law had a shadow

---

[36] ὕδωρ καθαρὸν, used in 10.22 for baptismal water, is an LXX term for the holy water of ritual cleansings; cf. Num. 5.17; Ez. 36.25.

of the good things to come, not the εἰκών itself of the things . . ."
(10.1). Paul spoke of the festivals, new moons, and sabbaths of the
Law as a shadow of the things to come (Col. 2.17), and Heb.'s
thought is like Paul's in so far as the ministrations and institutions
of the Law for both writers are given a role foreshadowing the
eschatological realities in the new time. But as we will note in the
paragraph, for Heb. the features of the old covenant are pre-
figurements of eschatology and at the same time earthly manifestations of eternal archetypes. In Philo's writings the relationship
between an eternal archetype and its earthly copy are frequently
described as that between an existent thing and the shadow it
throws.[37] In this figure Philo follows a common metaphor, but
best known from Plato's famous allegory of the cave (*Rep.* 514ff.),
according to which an inadequate expression of a thing is described
as a shadow over against the true reality which it represents in an
inferior way.[38] We have seen[39] how Philo asserted that the letters
of the Torah are "to the oracle but as the shadow to the substance
and that the higher values therein revealed are what really and
truly exist (τὰ ἀληθείᾳ πράγματα)" (*Conf.* 190). He meant that just as
one cannot come to the true knowledge of the world of archetypes
except through observing the sensible copies of those archetypes
as it were, their shadows, so one must start with the literal text
as an empirical shadow and then pass beyond it to the truth hidden
behind it. So Philo regarded the allegorical truths of scripture as
lying in an archetypal realm, τὰ ἀληθείᾳ πράγματα opposed to
the literal sense, the σκία.

The expression in Heb. 10.1 εἰκὼν τῶν πραγμάτων is Platonic as
well.[40] The Greek *eikon* sometimes carried the meaning of form"
in the sense of a diminution of the real thing, a "likeness,"[41] and
sometimes "form" designated the very "pattern" or "archtype"
of the thing.[42] Philo claims that the legislation of the Law is an
eikon of the νόμοι ἔμψυχοι, meaning by eikon "copy" or "like-

[37] See above p. 29f.
[38] At Heb. 10.1 Strack-Billerbeck note the rarity of the shadow metaphor
in rabbinic texts and when it occurs it does not speak of the shadow-reality
juxtaposition as here.
[39] See above p. 29f.
[40] See Moffatt.
[41] H. Kleinknecht, TWNT II, p. 386.
[42] Liddell-Scott. Although in Plato εἰκών was a technical word for "copy,"
nevertheless in Neo-Platonism flourishing at the time Heb. was written εἰκών

ness."[43] Heb. declares the Law does *not* have the *eikon* of the things, using the word in the second sense, meaning an archetype, for in 10.1 *eikon* is set over against the shadow which the Law admittedly had, in a way recalling Philo's σκια-ἀρχέτυπος schema. In Heb. it is asserted we must look beyond the Law for the archetypes (ἐικόνα), for the Law displays a mere copy (σκία). Thus, when Philo says the Law is an *eikon* or copy of another Law, and Heb. says it has a shadow of things to come, both are putting it on a level where its true meaning can only be seen as it represents something transcending itself and to which it is subordinate. By saying the Law has only a shadow of a truth lying beyond it, Heb. is saying nothing more about the Law than is uttered by Philo concerning the literal text of the Torah. But what is said by Philo to spare the Torah from discard as he presses on to profounder ideas underlying the shadow, is taken up by Heb. to compel the setting aside of the Torah precisely because it has *only* a shadow.

3: The Shadow of the Heavenly and Eschatological Cult

Both Philo and Heb. give much importance to the instructions in Ex. 25.40 to Moses concerning the sanctuary: "See that you make everything according to the pattern which was shown you on the mountain" (Heb. 8.5). The verse caused a good deal of speculation in late Judaism and early Christianity,[44] and Philo

---

became a synonym for ἰδέα and took on the meaning of "model." This Neo-Platonic usage is occasionally found in Philo; cf. Som. I 79; H. Willms, ειχων: *eine begriffsgeschichtliche Untersuchung zum Platonismus, Teil I: Philo von Alexandreia*, Münster, 1935, pp. 25–29. F. Eltester, *Eikon im Neuen Testament* (BZNW, 24), 1958, p. 8, explains that in this use the ideas were thought of as "invisible images."

[43] *Abr.* 3f.; *LA* III 96; *Praem.* 29; see above pp. 46–49.

[44] The basic notion behind it was a general oriental idea that every earthly sanctuary is a copy of a heavenly sanctuary; cf. W. Eichrodt, *Theology of the Old Testament* I, 1961, p. 423. *Wisd.* 9.8 states this prototype of the earthly tabernacle was created "from the beginning," and it was made one of the seven items created before the world in *Pesahim* 54a; cf. *Nedarim* 39b; *Midr. Ps.* 90.13, and other passages listed by H. Wenschkewitz, *op. cit.*, p. 48f. But elsewhere it was asserted that it merely came into God's thought before creation; *Gen. R.* 1.4; *Midr. Tehillim* on Ps. 93.2, 3, p. 207b; cf. H. Wolfson, *Philo* I, p. 182f. See also Acts 7.44; *Barn.* 6.11, 16.

found in it a support for his own Platonic concept that "every sense-perceptible likeness has (as) its origin an intelligible pattern in nature" (*QE* II 52; cf. I 19; *Opif.* 13, 34, 130; *Spec.* III 207; *Som.* I 206). He asserted on the basis of this passage that Moses in this experience was also given a mystic vision of the whole world of incorporeal ideas (*LA* III 96–103; *Som.* I 206; *Plant.* 27).

It is striking that although Heb. and Philo's citation of Ex. 25.40 differ respectively from our LXX copies, they coincide in citing the text so as to make a more general application of the idea expressed there, each adding πάντα.[45] This brief remark in Exodus was of apologetic value for Philo because it proved that Moses taught a basic Platonic doctrine centuries before Plato lived. But the very text which Philo used to Judaism's defence was turned in Heb. to its disadvantage. Heb. sees the text as a clear indication that Judaism is based upon an earthly cult all of whose institutions are mere copies of heavenly archetypes, a cult which is a *"ὑπόδειγμα* and shadow of the heavenly things" (8. 5).[46]

The first covenant had regulations for worship and an earthly or cosmic sanctuary in contrast to the heavenly one (9.1). In this earthly tabernacle with worship taking place in the first tent, the way into the second tent which is the holy of holies (9.3, 8f.) is not open. In the verses following the second tent and heaven are so interrelated that I feel their connection is that witnessed by Philo in which the holy of holies in the allegory of the tabernacle stood for heaven (*Spec.* I 66; *QE* II 91). The Jewish high priest's entrance into this holy place depicted the mystic soaring of the mind into heaven (*Som.* II 231–233; *Gig.* 52; *Mig.* 104). The writer intends to say that because the earthly sanctuary is only a copy of the heavenly one it can never bring anyone into the heavenly sanctuary, or into heaven itself. But one can be brought into heaven by a high priest who ascends into "the greater and more perfect tent . . . once for all into the sanctuary to obtain an eternal redemption"

---

[45] LXX: ὅρα ποιήσεις κατὰ τὸν τύπον τὸν δεδειγμένον σοι ἐν τῷ ὄρει; Heb. 8.5: ὅρα ποιήσεις πάντα κατὰ τὸν τύπον τὸν δειχθέντα σοι ἐν τῷ ὄρει; *LA* III 102: κατὰ τὸ παράδειγμα τὸ δεδειγμένον σοι ἐν τῷ ὄρει πάντα ποιήσεις. Here παράδειγμα and τύπος are, of course, synonyms, both meaning "pattern"; cf. J. H. Heyde, "Typus: Ein Beitrag zur Bedeutungsgeschichte des Wortes," in *Forschungen und Fortschritte*, 1941, p. 220.

[46] Like εἰκών, ὑπόδειγμα also had the double meaning pattern-copy; see Bauer's lexicon.

(9.11f.). After showing how Christ has performed this high priestly work, entering the heavenly sanctuary with his own blood in parallel fashion to the former high priests who entered the holy of holies with the blood of goats and bulls (9.12–14), the writer continues:

> It was necessary that the copies of the things in the heavens be cleansed by these rites, but the heavenly things by better sacrifices than these.[47] For Christ has not entered a sanctuary made with hands, an ἀντίτυπα τῶν ἀληθινῶν but into *heaven itself*, now to appear before God for us. (9.23f.)

Here the "antitype of the true sanctuary" appears simply as an earthly counterpart to heaven. The adjective ἀληθινός is of course used in the Platonic sense of a "true form" or pattern of an earthly thing,[48] just as in 8.1f. by way of preface to Ex. 25.40 the writer says Christ is seated as high priest "in the heavens, a minister of the sanctuary and of the true tabernacle (τῆς σκηνῆς τῆς ἀληθινῆς) which the Lord set up, not man."[49] So Heb. says now "by the blood of Jesus we have an entrance into the sanctuary. This entrance Jesus inaugurated for us as a new and living way

---

[47] While thinking that all the cultic articles and procedures are replicas of heavenly ones, Heb. has noted in vv. 18–23 that "almost all the cultic vessels were cleansed in blood" under the old dispensation. It is characteristic for the writer's thought that if one thing happened in the old covenant somehow it must also be matched with a like phenomenon in the new. So he even says that Christ has cleansed the heavenly articles by better sacrifices than Moses performed to cleanse the earthly ones. If M. Barth, *Was Christ's Death a Sacrifice*, Edinburgh, 1961, p. 47 n. 1, were right, "Hebrews speaks about sacrifice only in the light of Christ's sacrifice," the strange idea of Christ's cleansing of the elements of the heavenly cult with sacrifices (plural) surely would never have occurred to the writer. Jewish speculation endeavored to find a corresponding heavenly article or practice for every detail of the earthly cult, so on the Day of Atonement sacrifices in heaven take place in exactly the same way the high priest sacrifices. See H. Bietenhard, *Die himmlische Welt im Urchristentum und Spätjudentum*, Tübingen, 1951, pp. 124ff., for passages and a further discussion.

[48] R. Bultmann, TWNT I, p. 240.

[49] For τὰ ἀληθινὰ opposed to copies, see G. H. Whitaker, "ἀλήθεια in the New Testament and in Polybius," *The Expositor*, 1920, pp. 76–80, who illustrates the word from Polybius where the noun ἀλήθεια refers to the model of a ship to be built. C. H. Dodd, *The Interpretation of the Fourth Gospel*, Cambridge, 1953, p. 177f., thinks ἀλήθεια in John rests on truth as ultimate reality, eternal and standing above the phenomenal world.

($\dot{o}\delta\dot{o}\varsigma$) through the curtain. This he did through his flesh."[50]
E. Käsemann deserves credit for having compared the $\dot{o}\delta\dot{o}\varsigma$ here
to the $\dot{o}\delta\dot{o}\varsigma$ which for Philo leads through the cosmos to the
heavenly world.[51] This road, called $\dot{\eta}$ $\beta\alpha\sigma\iota\lambda\iota\varkappa\dot{\eta}$ $\dot{o}\delta\dot{o}\varsigma$ in Philo's
allegory of Num. 20.17–20 (Immut. 144; 150–163; Post. 101 f.), is
a means of God's grace. Philo puts the following words in God's
mouth:

> I do this in pity for rational nature, that it may be caused to rise out of the
> nether region of the passions into the upper region of virtue guided step
> by step by Me, Who have laid down the road that leads to heaven and
> appointed it as a highway for all suppliant souls, that they might not grow
> weary as they treat it (Post. 31; cf. Immut. 142–163; 182; Mig. 171).

Heb. says the Hodos from earth to heaven, which for Philo was
the Hodos of Sophia (Immut. 143; 160), was not yet revealed so
long as worship was confined to an earthly sanctuary (9.8), and
is not open now in Judaism, bound as it is to mere copies of
heavenly things.[52]

But there appears to be another nuance in the term $\ddot{\alpha}\gamma\iota o\nu$
$\varkappa o\sigma\mu\iota\varkappa\dot{o}\nu$ as well (9.1). It suggests the writer was thinking of the
cosmic symbolism of the temple as expounded by Josephus and
Philo. Spicq thinks a cosmic symbolism reference is impossible
since the writer is speaking of the tabernacle and not the Herodian
temple in Jerusalem. However Spicq overlooks the fact that Philo
and Josephus based their descriptions of the Jerusalem temple
with its symbolism upon the tabernacle as it is portrayed in
Exodus.[53] Furthermore Wisd. 9.8 treats the Jerusalem temple as a
replica of the tabernacle.[54] That the writer means "the tabernacle

---

[50] I agree with Spicq that $\tau o\tilde{\upsilon}\tau$ $\ddot{\epsilon}\sigma\tau\iota\nu$ $\tau\tilde{\eta}\varsigma$ $\sigma\alpha\rho\varkappa\dot{o}\varsigma$ $\alpha\dot{\upsilon}\tau o\tilde{\upsilon}$ does not identify
the curtain, for the latter is elsewhere (6.19; 9.3) not a means of access but
a barrier to entrance, similar to the curtain's symbolizing the separation
between the higher and lower spheres in Philo (QE II 91). This barrier has been
broken by means of Christ's sacrifice. The preposition $\delta\iota\dot{\alpha}$ governs the geni-
tives $\tau o\tilde{\upsilon}$ $\varkappa\alpha\tau\alpha\pi\epsilon\tau\dot{\alpha}\sigma\mu\alpha\tau o\varsigma$ and $\tau\tilde{\eta}\varsigma$ $\sigma\alpha\rho\varkappa\dot{o}\varsigma$, but the first refers to place, and the
second to means. N. Dahl, "A New and Living Way," Interpretation, 1951,
p. 405, offers another plausible interpretation, that the flesh of Jesus is identi-
cal with the curtain in its double aspect of hiding the true sanctuary in heaven
and at the same time making the entrance to it possible.

[51] Op. cit., pp. 50 ff.

[52] See above p. 95 f.

[53] See above p. 57 f.

[54] "Thou hast given command to build a temple on thy holy mountain,
and an altar in the city of thy habitation, a copy of the holy tent which thou

with its cosmic symbolism" in 9.1 seems further substantiated by the articles he lists in 9.2–5 belonging to it which were allegorized by Philo to represent parts of the world's structure. The lamp-stands depict the heavens and the planets (*QE* II 73 ff.; *Mos.* II 102 f.). The table and the bread of the presence is the whole animal world, "since loaves ... which creatures needing food must use, are placed on it" (*Her.* 226; *Mos.* II 104). The holy of holies stands for heaven, and its curtain refers to the separation of the lower and upper parts of the cosmos (*QE* II 91). The altar of incense with its various parts represent the four elements of the cosmos, earth, fire, air, and water (*Her.* 226).[55] In one form of the allegory the Cherubim standing above the mercy seat of the ark represent the two hemispheres (*Mos.* II 97 f.).[56] The ark's being made of pure gold within and simply gold without refers to the world of incorporeal things and the outward visible world (*QE* II 54).

As we showed earlier, this symbolic interpretation of the taber-nacle in Philo and Josephus apparently was to answer the Hellen-istic charge that Judaism had bound a spiritual God to one place by having a temple when the whole world is God's temple. The Hellenistic Jews answered this indictment by saying it is as men look to the temple's (actually the tabernacle's) cosmic representa-tion that they learn the truth that the world is God's temple. But

---

didst prepare from the beginning." Philo says the tabernacle was a "portable temple;" *QE* II 83; *Mos.* II 73.

[55] O. Moe, "Das irdische und das himmlische Heiligtum," *Theologische Zeitschrift*, 1953, p. 25 f., thinks the reason why the writer has moved the altar of incense from its place outside (Ex. 30.6) to within the holy of holies is because burnt offerings are sometimes a symbol of prayer (Ps. 141.2; Rev. 8.3 f.), and he wants to show that now Christians are allowed to go forward to the throne of grace with their prayers (cf. 10.22; 4.16). This interpretation would agree nicely with what we have been saying about the parallelism of the features of the two covenants, for it would show a new phenomenon anticipated in the structure of the old cult. But in v. 6 the writer has the priests continually offering outside the holy of holies, presupposing that the altar is in its proper place, So I do not believe he means to show anything by this slip, just as he has no profound reflection for placing the golden urn, the manna, and Aaron's rod all *in* the ark (v. 4).

[56] After the above description the writer says he cannot speak about all the details of the tabernacle, or perhaps of the ark, that is, κατὰ μέρος, v. 5. But after a detailed description and allegory of the ark in a Greek fragment to *QE* II 68 Philo says, τὰ μὲν οὖν περὶ τὴν κιβωτὸν κατὰ μέρος εἴρηται.

Heb. says, although the sanctuary or temple may have symbolized the cosmos as the Jewish apologists claimed, this still does not correct a fundamental flaw in it, namely that it is "made with hands," χειροποίητος. Philo himself had referred to the temple as χειρόκμητος (*Mos.* II 88), over against the "highest, and in the truest sense the holy, temple of God . . . the whole universe" (*Spec.* I 66f.). Heb. brings up Hellenism's criticism against all temples "made with hands." To emphasize the point that Christ entered no tabernacle "made with hands," such as that of the first covenant, the writer says that Christ has become a high priest, having gone "through the better and more perfect tabernacle, not made with hands, that is, not of this creation" (9.11); "for Christ did not enter into a sanctuary made with hands, an antitype of the true one, but into heaven itself" (v. 24).

The writer actually thinks that Judaism has committed idolatrous practices in its sanctuary made with hands,[57] so he says the Jews "worship a copy and shadow of the heavenly things" (5.5), and calls them "they who worship the tabernacle" (13.10).[58] Whether he says that the Jews worship the articles of their cult because he feels they have misdirected their worship to the copies of the heavenly things revealed by God (Ex. 25.40; Heb. 8.5), or because he regards as amounting to idolatry the adherence to the earthly cult made with hands in the time when the new high priest has ascended into the heavenly sanctuary, is not clear.

We showed above[59] how Heb. employs the technical allegorical term found in Philo, ὑπόδειγμα, and in 4.11 uses it to show a typal

---

[57] χειροποίητος was a term often describing idolatry. In the LXX χειροποίητος was used to translate *elil*; Is. 2.18; 16.12; 19.1; 21.9; 31.7. M. Simon, *op. cit.*, p. 89 n. 27, says, "It thus not only describes idols, it is synonymous with 'idol.'" He also remarks that in Stephen's speech the Jerusalem temple and the golden calf are described "made with hands" (Acts 7. 47), and "works of their hands" (71.4) respectively. *Sib. Or.* 604–6 laments men "reverenced and honoured idols made by men's hands . . ."; cf. 6.18. *Wisd.* 13.10 says, "But miserable, with their hopes set on dead things, are the men who give the name 'gods' to the works of men's hands . . ."; cf. 14.8. The synonym χειρόκμητος is applied to idols by Philo (*Post.* 166; *Legat.* 290; *Dec.* 76).

[58] Bauer in his lexicon sets a special usage of λατρεύω in these passages, i.e., to worship by means of the cultic objects. He gives no parallels or other support for this refinement. Related to 13.10 would be *Diognetus* III–IV where all Jewish worship is regarded as idolatry.

[59] P. 96f.

relationship in a parenetic application of a Biblical incident to the new period of *Heilsgeschichte*. The typological meaning is still retained when Heb. speaks of the earthly copies, ὑποδείγματα, of the heavenly cult (8.5; 9.23). While the elements of the earthly cult are for Heb. impressions of prototypes in heaven, nevertheless the rites which take place in the earthly sanctuary are not duplications of simultaneous procedures in heaven. Rather the earthly sacrifices are anticipations of Christ's "once for all" sacrificial work "at the end of the age." Heb. emphatically denies that Christ was sacrificing himself in heaven all the time the sacrifices were carried out in the cult modelled after the heavenly one (9.25f.; 7.27). The writer not only shows the idealistic relation of the heavenly and earthly cult, he also arranges the two in the typological parallel of the two dispensations. C. K. Barrett[60] rightly says:

> The heavenly tabernacle and its ministrations are from one point of view eternal archetypes, from another, they are eschatological events.

The author tries to show that certain features of the earthly cult reflect prototypes in heaven while the sacrifices within them foreshadow features of Christ's work accomplished later in history. The high priest who went within the veil to perform sacrificial rites[61] anticipated Christ our forerunner who later penetrated the veil in heaven (10.20; 9.11, 24) where he carried our hope as an anchor of our souls (6.19f.; cf. Lev. 16.2). The sprinkled blood of goats and bulls (Lev. 16.3, 14) finds its counterpart in the blood of Christ (9.13f., cf. vv. 23, 24). As the high priest brought blood into the holy of holies with him (Lev. 16.2, 14; Heb. 9.7, 25), so Christ entered the heavenly holy of holies with his own blood (9.12). Just as the old covenant was inaugurated (ἐγκεκαίνισται) with blood (9.18), so the new covenant, or "new and living way," was inaugurated (ἐγκεκαίνισται) by the blood of Christ (10.19f.). In both cases the blood involved is called "the blood of the covenant" (9.20; 10.29), applying a phrase from Ex. 24.8 to the new as well as the old covenant. Having pointed out that the animal blood and the blood of Christ were brought into the respective

---

[60] "The Eschatology of the Epistle to the Hebrews," in *The Background of the New Testament and its Eschatology*, Cambridge, 1956, p. 385.

[61] The ἐισερχομένην εἰς τὸ ἐσώτερον τοῦ καταπετάσματος of 6.19 is an allusion to Aaron's high priestly instruction about when to go behind the veil, εἰσπορευέσθω ... εἰς τὸ ἅγιον ἐσώτερον τοῦ καταπετάσματος (Lev. 16.2).

sanctuaries, the writer notes that the bodies of the animals were burned outside the camp (Lev. 16.27), anticipating something else in Jesus' work: "So Jesus also suffered outside the gate in order to sanctify the people through his blood" (13.11f.). Thus the sanctuary and its elements which are ὑποδείγματα, copies of true ones in heaven, are nevertheless arranged in the typological relationship of the two covenants, for the sacrifices transpiring within them foreshadow in careful detail the various circumstances in Christ's sacrifice.

4: Perfection of the Covenant

In the passage 5.11–6.3 the τελείοι are those who have achieved the "mature doctrine" (τελειότης, 6.1), which is the Christological exegesis of the O.T. As we saw above, the τελείοι contrasted with the νήπιοι comes from Hellenistic school terminology, and the meaning of perfection in this passage is closer to the word's usage in Philo than anywhere else in the letter.[62] J. Kögel[63] called attention to the wide range covered by τελειοῦν and related terms in the secular and Biblical vocabulary, and concluded that it is a very general expression, its exact meaning being decided by the context. Throughout the letter the writer is under the influence of Lev. 16, the rites of the Day of Atonement, which he fits into a typological schema anticipating Christ's sacrifice. Evidently the notion of perfection in connection with Christ's priestly work came to his mind when he read the specifications, "The priest shall propitiate, whomever they anoint and whomever's hands they

---

[62] See above p. 78f. Philo thought of ethical philosophy as an ascetic climb through stages of discipline finally to perfection. The necessary ingredients to perfection were teaching, nature, and practice (ἄσκησις). Scripture symbolizes the exponents of all these as Abraham, Isaac and Jacob respectively (Abr. 53). When the learner has at last attained to Sophia, he becomes a τέλειος (Mut. 270; Som. II 234–236; LA II 91; III 140; 144; 207. On the τέλειος man according to Philo, see W. Völker, op. cit., pp. 260ff. As we study the passages other than 5.14 and 6.1, however, the discrepancy between Philo's philosophical interpretation of perfection and that found in Heb. will become apparent.

[63] "Der Begriff τελειοῦν im Hebräerbrief," Theologische Studien Martin Kähler zum 6. Januar 1905 dargebracht, Leipzig, 1905, pp. 38ff.

consecrate (τελειώσουσιν τὰς χεῖρας)[64] to serve as priest after his father . . ." (Lev. 16.32 LXX). Because the former high priest was consecrated or perfected, so Christ the new high priest must be perfected as well. Since the writer sees Christ's being perfected in connection with his suffering, i.e., his vicarious self-offering for the sins of the people (2.10; 5.8-10), it seems reasonable that he thought of this perfection in typological relation to the τελείωσις of sacrificial victims in the Pentateuch (Ex. 29.22, 26, 27, 31, 34; Lev. 8.22, 28, 29, 31, 37).

But in Heb. the meaning of perfection at once expands beyond the sphere of the cultic consecration of a priest and offering. The writer differentiates between the Son who has been made perfect and the former high priests whom the Law appointed who had weaknesses, and thereby links the idea of Christ's perfection as high priest with that of his sinlessness (7.28), since ἀσθένεια in Heb. denotes a proneness to sin (4.15; 5.2). Then he denies that there was any perfection through the Levitical priesthood (7.11), and states that the Law on which this priesthood was based "made nothing perfect (7.19; 9.9; 10.1). By now it is obvious that the author is working with a much larger concept of perfection than he started with in the Pentateuch passages which spoke of the consecrated or perfected high priest and the τελείωσις of the offerings.

This is because Heb. has incorporated the concept of perfection into the theology of the two covenants. So applied perfection means, *the bringing to completion in the new covenant of that which was anticipated in the old.*[65] The concept in this way receives an eschatological significance as "the perfect" which will come according to 1 Cor. 13.10, and the τελείωσις or fulfillment of the divine promises in Lk. 1.45, and the type of Isaac τελεσθῇ in Christ (*Barn.* 7.3). With the exception of the special usage already noted in 5.14 and 6.1, perfection in its various applications in Heb. has behind it the thought that the typological features of the

---

[64] E. Riggenbach, "Der Begriff der τολείωσις im Hebräerbrief," *Neue Kirchliche Zeitschrift*, 1923, p. 186, translates: "whomever they consecrate with respect to the hands," i.e., to consecrate for his priestly activity. For the same expression see Ex. 29.29; 33.35; Lev. 4.5; 8.33; 16.32; 21.10; Num. 3.3.

[65] Similarly, J. Van der Ploeg, "L'exégèse de l'Ancien Testament dans l'épître aux Hébreux, RB, 1947, p. 189.

old covenant find their respective counterparts in the new covenant which brings the old to completion, that is, to perfection. The following considerations confirm this observation.

The heavenly tabernacle, which at once is an archetype of the earthly one and also is involved in Christ's eschatological work (8.2; 9.24), is called "the greater and *more perfect* tabernacle," as opposed to the earthly one made with hands, belonging to the former dispensation (9.11). The more perfect sanctuary complements and brings to consummation that of the old covenant. Again, Jesus, "the perfecter of the faith" (12.2), has brought to completion the sacrifices of the old covenant by his sacrifice. For the sacrifices of the old order are not able to perfect the conscience (9.9; 10.1) in the sense of cleansing it (9.14). But Christ's sacrifice does what the old sacrifices aimed at, bringing them to completion by cleansing the heart from a bad conscience (10.22) so that Christ has "perfected for all time by one offering those who are sanctified") (10.14).

In the treatise in which his eschatology is fully worked out, *On Rewards and Punishments*, Philo states that in the last days when Israel is gathered together in Palestine the patriarchs of the nation will intercede with God in behalf of the people,

> ... because with souls released from their bodies they show forth in that naked simplicity their devotion to their Ruler, and cease not to make supplication for their sons and daughters, supplications not made in vain, because the Father grants to them the privilege that their prayers should be heard (*Praem.* 166).

Thus Philo makes the salvation of the present Israel dependent upon that of the saints of old.[66] But in Heb. the thought is just the reverse. The fate of the O.T. heroes of faith, whose exploits are related in Heb. 11, is stated at the end of that chapter to be linked with the salvation of the new people of God: "God had foreseen something better for us, that apart from us they should not be made perfect" (11.40).[67] Salvation is fully possible only in

---

[66] That the departed righteous men effect reconciliation and atonement for Israel was a Jewish idea and not original to Philo. Elijah, identified with Phinehas (*Sifre* 131 to Num. 25.13), was said to atone for sins until the resurrection, See H. Kosmala, *op. cit.*, p. 81. Cohn, *Philos Werke*, cites *Midr. Schemot R. c.* 44 as parallel to this passage.

[67] Some commentators have understood μὴ χωρὶς ἡμῶν here simply to mean "not before us;" see Spicq's summary. But we prefer to take it as Riggenbach, "not excluding us."

the new covenant (11.13, 39). But because the people of God under the old covenant were the counterparts of those saved under the new, as the features of the old covenant are brought to completion or perfection in the new, the spirits of the old believers are "perfected," thus redeemed, along with those of the new believers. Thus, the new believers are reminded that they have come to the heavenly Jerusalem, "And to the assembly of the first-born enrolled in heaven, and to God the judge of all, and *to the spirits of just men made perfect*, and to Jesus, mediator of a new covenant" (12.22–24). The "something better" (11.40) which God foresaw must refer to the completion of salvation wrought by Christ.[68]

5: Old Testament Types of Christ

So far we have observed how the Law and cult find their parallels in the typology of the two covenants. In our definition of typology we said that persons in Biblical history also become types anticipating later persons, or antitypes. In Heb. certain personalities in the old covenant find their new covenant counterpart in Christ.

A: Moses and Christ:

The Mishnah shows the effort to find a type of the Messiah in Moses.[69] This interest in the Moses-Messiah typology perhaps would be of uncertain importance for the N.T. were it not for the fact that the *Damascus Document*, contemporary with the N.T. and considerably earlier than the Midrash, points clearly to the idea that the experience of Israel in the wilderness under Moses' leadership was an anticipation of the situation immediately before the Messianic age.[70] Josephus indicates that popular Messianic

---

[68] κρείττων often modifies the qualities of the new dispensation, see 7.19, 22; 8.6; 9.23.

[69] *Pesiq* 49b states that, as the first redeemer, Moses, so also the last redeemer, the Messiah, first will reveal and then hide himself. As Moses was raised in the court of Pharaoh so the Messiah will stay in Rome, the enemy city, before he appears publicly. See for further illustrations, Strack-Billerbeck I, p. 69f.; 86.

[70] The Covenanters lived in camps patterned after those of Israel's time in the wilderness (*Dam.* 19.2; cf. Deut. 7.9). Leaders were set over them in the pattern of Ex. 18.25 (*Dam.* 2.23). The connection with the Moses-Messiah typology of the Midrash seems clear. *Pirqe Maschiach Beth. ha-Midr.* 3.72.1

figures repeatedly arose who called out the people "into the wilderness."[71] So the typology of Moses of the Messiah was in Judaism during N.T. times, and it was natural therefore that in the early church Moses should be frequently a type of Christ.[72]

Heb. represents the same notion in early Christianity, drawing a typological parallel between Moses as the founder of the old covenant and Christ the founder of the new. The writer compares Moses and Christ, alluding to the phrase, Moses was "faithful in all his (God's) house" (Num. 12.7; Heb. 3.2). To appreciate the writer's comparison of Christ, "faithful to him who appointed[73] him" (v. 2), and Moses, faithful in God's house, we must first disassociate the remark "whose house we are" (3.6) from the preceeding passage, for it is an afterthought suggested to the writer probably by the Christian community's application of the house of God metaphor to the Church (1 Pet. 4.17; 1 Tim. 3.15; cf. Eph. 2.19–22; 1 Pet. 2.5).[74]

---

says, as Moses lead the people in the wilderness and did miracles so the Messiah will do the same. Strack-Billerbeck IV, p. 798; also II 284. The thought goes back to Hos. 2.16–19; 12.10. The idea that the time of Moses in the wilderness was the norm for Israelitic religion is, of course, much older. See H. Gressmann, *Der Messias*, Göttingen, 1929, pp. 181–183.

[71] *Bell.* II 259, 261; VI 351; VII 438. Recall the "Egyptian" who in Acts 21.38 lead 4000 into the wilderness. When anyone says the Messiah is "in the wilderness," Jesus warns not to go out (Mt. 24.26); J. Jeremias, TWNT IV, p. 866 n. 173.

[72] The expectation of Deut. 18.15 that in the last days God would raise up a prophet like Moses is applied to Jesus in Acts 3.22ff.; 7.37. Jesus' feeding the multitude in the wilderness, similar to the eating of the manna in the wilderness, seems to remind the people of Deut. 18.15 in Jn. 6.14. At other passages Moses and Christ are compared (Jn. 3.14; Rev. 15.3f.), and this comparison seems to have influenced the Gospel tradition; cf. Mk. 1.13; Mt. 4.2 (Ex. 34.28; Deut. 9.9, 18); 2.16 (Ex. 1.22); 2.20 (Ex. 4.19).

[73] Rather than the Vulgate, *creatori suo;* for ποιέω meaning to appoint someone to a position, as in the context, apostle and high priest, cf. Acts 2.36; 2 Cor. 5.21; Rev. 1.6; Mt. 4.19; Mk. 3.14.

[74] It scarcely needs to be mentioned that the writer is not thinking of the Church when Moses is placed in the house (3.2–5). 3.6 is a transition thought to pass from Moses' and Christ's faithfulness to the parenetic section following (3.7–4.13). The transitions of Heb. generally hang on a "hook-word" *mot-crochet)* which indicate the following topic; see L. Vaganay, "Le plan de l'épître aux Hébreux," in *Mémorial Lagrange*, Paris, 1940, pp. 269–277. In v. 6 that which hooks the previous discussion on the "house of God" with the next section is the admonition to "hold fast the confidence." In the transition the figure of the "house of God" takes on a parenetic meaning,

Heb. 3.2, 5 is the only N.T. reference to Num. 12.7, but it is by no means insignificant that it was a favorite passage of Philo, cited by him no less than four times (*LA* II 67; III 103, 204, 228). In each of these passages the text is cited in eulogy of Moses faithfulness. What is meant by "the house" is not explained. But in Hellenism the world was sometimes referred to as a house.[75] Philo says: "What would the visible house of God be except this world?" (*Post.* 5); "this world discerned by sense, is, as I now know, nothing but a house of 'God'" (*Som.* I 185); "The world, we read, is God's house in the realm of sense-perception" (*Plant.* 50). By the argument from design Philo asserted that the house-like universe must have its builder, God, just as every house must have a builder:

> Should a man see a house carefully constructed with a gateway, colonades, men's quarters, women's quarters, and the other buildings, he will get an idea of the artificer, for he will be of opinion that the house never reached that completeness without the skill of the craftsmen ... Just so anyone entering this world, as it were some vast house or city, and beholding the sky ... , planets and fixed stars ... , water and air ... , living creatures..., he will surely argue that these have not been wrought without consummate art, but that the Maker of this whole universe was and is God (*LA* III 98 f.; cf. *Cher.* 127).

The author of Heb. seems to have these notions in mind when he says that a house never is without a builder and then goes on to say that in the same way God is the builder of the universe, ὁ πάντα κατασκευάσας (v. 4). κατασκευάζω is, of course, a Biblical term for God's creative activity,[76] and when the writer says, "Yet Jesus has been counted worthy of as much more glory than Moses as the builder (ὁ κατασκευάσας) of a house has more honor than the house" (v. 3), Windisch's suggestion that he means by "house," "the world," seems probable. Heb., it appears, is familiar with the thought of the universe as the house of God. If the term "house of God" in Gen. 28.17 could be interpreted by Philo to refer to the world (*Som.* I 185), the same phrase could be so interpreted in Num. 12.7—either in one of Philo's lost treatises or by other

anticipating the Parenesis in 3.7–4.16. Cf. the next transition containing the "hook-word" "high priest," linking with the next part, and "confidence," tying with the proceeding (4.14–16).

[75] O. Michel, TWNT V, p. 125.
[76] Is. 40.28; 45.7; *Wisd.* 9.2; 11.24; 13.4; *Bar.* 3.32.

exegetes in the Jewish Alexandrian school. According to a natural Alexandrian exegesis, Moses in Num. 12.7 would be praised for being faithful in God's creation.

In his typology of Moses of Christ Heb. takes for granted that this is what is meant in the text. But the writer wants to emphasize now the difference between Moses' faithfulness and Christ's. Moses was faithful as a "servant in testimony of the things to be revealed later," whereas Christ is faithful "as a son over his (God's) house" (v. 6). Christ is *over* ($\dot{\varepsilon}\pi\iota$) the creation in contrast to Moses. In the previous chapter the writer had interpreted Ps. 8.5-7 Christologically, since its claim that all creation has been placed in subjection under man's feet only applies to Christ (2.6-8). The psalm also contains the words, "thou hast crowned him with glory and honor," which the writer exposits in 2.9. On the basis of Ps. 8 placing Christ over creation, the writer says of the "glory and honor" of Christ, "Jesus has been considered worthy of more glory than Moses as the builder of the house has more honor than the house" (v. 3). Heb. is trying to demonstrate that Christ, the fulfiller of Ps. 8, has more glory and honor than Moses, because he is over the creation (v. 6). The creation is subject to him (2.8)— indeed he is its maker ($\dot{o}$ $\varkappa\alpha\tau\alpha\sigma\varkappa\varepsilon\nu\dot{\alpha}\sigma\alpha\varsigma$ $\alpha\dot{\upsilon}\tau\dot{o}\nu$, v. 3; cf. 1.2, 10-12; 2.10). Because of the congregation's danger of apostasy into Judaism the writer is careful to show how Christ is greater than Moses his type.

Another passage in Heb. states that Moses refused to be regarded as Pharoah's daughter's son, "choosing rather to be mistreated with the people of God than to have the temporary pleasure of sin, considering the reproach of Christ greater reward than the treasures of Egypt" (11.25f.). Jewish writers sometimes pictured Moses as a great sufferer "who suffered many things in Egypt and in the Red Sea and in the wilderness during forty years" (*Ass. Mos.* 3.11).[77] Heb. recalls this, but finds in Moses' suffering disgrace an anticipation of the reviling Christ suffered, and so alludes to the phrase $\tau\dot{o}\nu$ $\dot{o}\nu\varepsilon\iota\delta\iota\sigma\mu\dot{o}\nu$ $\tau o\tilde{\upsilon}$ $X\varrho\iota\sigma\tau o\tilde{\upsilon}$ (Ps. 89.51).

[77] If A. Bentzen, *Messias, Moses redivivus, Menschensohn*, Zurich, 1948, is right, this emphasis could be as old as Deutero-Isaiah. Bentzen argues that the Suffering Servant of the Lord is actually a Messianic figure and a new Moses. However that may be, it must be granted Bentzen (p. 65) that there are Pentateuch passages in which Moses appears ready to suffer vicariously for the people. Cf. Ex. 32.32; Deut. 4.21; 9.17-20.

If the benediction in 13.20f. was not a formula already in the Christian tradition before the writer used it, it also contains the typology of Moses of Christ. Is. 63.11f. LXX speaking of God says:

And he who brought the shepherd of the sheep (τὸν ποιμένα τῶν προβάτων) up out of the land remembered the eternal days. Where is he who placed the Holy Spirit in them, who brought (ὁ ἀγαγῶν) Moses by his right hand,[78] the hand of his glory?

Because Moses was for the writer a type of Christ he applies phrases from this Moses passage to Christ. He begins the benediction, "And the God of peace, who brought again (ἀναγαγὼν) from the dead the great shepherd of the sheep (τὸν ποιμένα τῶν προβάτων) . . ."

B: The Priestly Types of Christ:

While it is not a suggestion entirely wanting in late Judaism or elsewhere in the primitive church, Heb.'s idea of Christ's work as a priestly one is original and unique in the N.T.[79] Priesthood has

---

[78] Is it possible that the author read Τῇ δεξιᾷ as a locative and not instrumental, so that Moses was brought *to* the right hand of God? In that case the phrase must have called to the writer's mind Ps. 110.1 which he interpreted Christologically (1.3, 13; 8.1; 10.12; 12.2) and that would have been enough to place the passage in the Moses typology of Christ. Perhaps he saw here a reference to the assumption of Moses, parallel to Christ's resurrection.

[79] That the Messiah would be a priest is asserted in *Test. Sim.* 7.1–3, and it is well-known that the Qumran sect expected a priestly Messiah (of Aaron) and a lay Messiah (of Israel). See K. G. Kuhn, "The Two Messiahs of Aaron and Israel," in *The Scrolls and the New Testament*, New York, 1957, ed. K. Stendahl, pp. 54–64. C. Spicq, "L'origine johannique de la conception du Christ-prêtre dans l'épître aux Hébreux," in *Aux sources de la tradition chrétienne, Mélanges M. Goguel*, Neuchâtel, 1950, pp. 258–269, tried to show that the idea was developed in Heb. from Johannine theology, but he succeeded only in establishing that for John the O.T. cult has been transposed to Christ's person. John's interest in Christ's purification of the temple is not found in Heb. 5.7 (p. 260); the only purification of the earthly sanctuary spoken of in Heb. (9.23) has to do with Moses' and not Christ's priestly work which purifies the heavenly things. Spicq's assertion (p. 265) that John as well as Heb. shows attention for Christ's ministry as priest in the heavenly temple is given without support. O. Moe, "Das Priestertum Christi im Neuen Testament ausserhalb des Hebräerbriefs," TL, 1947, col. 335–338, finds a significant number of priestly concepts applied to Christ in Rev., 1 Pet., and Rom. as well as in Heb.

seemed to some an odd Christological category to choose,[80] but it is understandable how the notion came to the writer's mind and thence passed into the Christian tradition[81] for he read the title "priest" in v. 4 of the Christologically understood Ps. 110: "The Lord has sworn and will not change his mind. 'Thou art a priest forever after the order of Melchizedek.' "[82]

But why Ps. 110.4 particularly struck the writer's eye seems due to his Alexandrian background and anti-Judaic debate. For although the passage contains the recurrent title "priest" (7.3, 11, 14, 15, 20; 8.4; 10.11), it does not contain the even more important one, "high priest."[83] We saw than an apology for their religion among the Hellenistic Jews found in Philo and Josephus tried to show Judaism as the universal religion *par excellence* through an interpretation of the high priest's garments. The universe was symbolized on these garments so that the whole cosmos could accompany the high priest in his rituals (*Mos.* II 133). Furthermore, unlike all other national religious figures, the Jewish high priest offered prayers for all mankind (*Spec.* I 97). In his mediatorship for the whole human race the high priest approached the position of the Logos which he depicted allegorically and which also acted as mediator between God and man. Thus, the high priest became for Philo a semi-divine being, midway between divinity and humanity (*Spec.* I 116).[84] So just as it was necessary for Heb. to answer the apology for the "cosmic sanctuary" as well as to show its typological meaning, so it was also necessary to indicate why Christ was above as well as like his priestly types, not only as portrayed in the O.T. but also as seen by Hellenistic Judaism, because this expression of Judaism had picked the high priest as the locus for its self-vindication. This

---

[80] So MacNeill, *op. cit.*, p. 30; Scott, *op. cit.*, p. 128f. F. Büchsel, *Die Christologie des Hebräerbriefs*, Gütersloh, 1922, p. 74, tried to establish all Heb.'s statements about Christ in the category of sonship instead.

[81] *Ignatius Phil.* 9.1; 1 *Clem.* 36.1; 61.3; 64.1; *Polycarp Phil.* 12.2; *Martyrdom of Polycarp* 14.3.

[82] So C.H. Dodd, *According to the Scriptures*, p. 122; O. Michel, commentary, p. 83, recognizes this text as the kernel for Heb. 7, and Windisch sees it notably behind 5.10; 6.20; 7.1–10.18.

[83] 2.17; 3.1; 4.14, 15; 5.1, 5; 6.20; 7.26, 27, 28; 8.1, 3; 9.7, 11, 25.

[84] See above p. 61f.

explains the interchange of terms "priest" and "high priest" in Heb.[85]

To be a merciful and faithful high priest Christ had to be like his brethren (2.17f.), therefore he became incarnate (2.14). Thus the high priest may treat the ignorant and wayward with proper compassion, that is, to have μετριοπαθεῖν toward them (5.2). μετριοπαθεῖν was a philosophical term referring to the proper mean between excessive passion and apathy[86] and is used as such by Philo.[87] Such would seem to be a strange quality to attribute to a high priest, but it is important for Heb. 5.2 that Philo assigns this disposition to Aaron the high priest at Ex. 28.30, whose moderate passion is, however, differentiated from the removal of all passion observed in the wise man Moses:

> Well, Aaron, as I have said, having this passion, attempts to cure it by the saving medicines that have been mentioned. Moses, on the other hand, thinks it necessary to use the knife on the seat of anger in its entirety, and to cut it clean out of the soul, for no μετριοπάθεια can satisfy him (*LA* III 129; cf. 134).

Aaron appears as the exponent of μετριοπαθεῖν again at *LA* III 134. Inasmuch as both Philo and Heb. attest to μετριοπάθεια being a quality of the high priest, it seems that this was regarded in the Alexandrian school as a proper disposition in him. Heb. asserts that Christ fulfills this high priestly qualification because of his genuine humanity and suffering this entailed (5.2, 7–9).

Still remembering the δόξα and τιμή with which God crowned Christ in Ps. 8.5–7 (2.7), the writer sets up another typological parallel between the high priesthood of Aaron and of Christ in commenting on these two terms. No high priest usurps the *honor* of the high priest. Christ did not *glorify* himself but was called by God just as Aaron, which is seen in God's appointing Christ in Ps. 2.7 and 110.4 (5.4–6.10).

---

[85] Rather than that the writer is combining an early Christian tradition of Christ's priesthood with the idea of the high priest *homologia*, as G. Schille, "Erwägungen zur Hohenpriesterlehre des Hebräerbriefes," ZNW, 1955, pp. 81 ff.

[86] See Windisch.

[87] So at Sarah's death Abraham did not "grieve over-bitterly as at an utterly new and unheard-of misfortune, nor yet assume an indifference (ἀπαθεία) as though nothing painful had occurred, but choose the mean rather than the extremes," μετριοπαθεῖν (*Abr.* 257; cf. *Jos.* 26).

Jesus and the former high priests are both appointed "with reference to what concerns God" (τὰ πιρὸς τὸν θεόν, 2.17; 5.1), the latter to make offerings and sacrifices for sins (5.1; 8.3), and the former "to make expiation for the sins of the people" (2.17).

That Christ is "separated from sinners" (7.26) probably is meant to parallel the former high priests' custom of staying eight days in the temple before the Day of Atonement to meditate on their cultic purity.[88]

The N.T. doctrine of Christ's intercession for us before the Father (Rom. 8.34; 1 Jn. 2.1) as Heb. applies it to Christ's high priesthood (7.25; 9.24) seems to answer to the intercession of the Jewish high priest on behalf of all mankind as described in Philo's apology (*Spec.* I 116; *Her.* 205f.; *Spec.* I 97; *Mos.* II 5; *Praem.* 56).

But the parallel between the old and new high priest is not perfect in Heb. because the former high priest was a sinner (5.3; 7.27), while the new one was tempted as we but "without sinning" (4.15). The N.T. doctrine of Christ's sinlessness (2 Cor. 5.21; Jn. 1.47; 8.46; 1 Pet. 1.19; 2.22) applied to the high priest seems especially important in view of Philo's statements about the high priest. Following the LXX distinction between intentional (ἐκουσία) and unintentional sins (ἀκούσια),[89] Philo says, "But the high priest has concern neither with voluntary nor with involuntary sins, remaining far above them both" (*Fug.* 115; cf. 117; 108; *Spec.* I 228–230; 243; III 134f.).[90] Heb. says further, "It was fitting that we should have such a high priest, holy, blameless, unstained (ἀμίαντος) . . ." (9.26). ἀμίαντος was not applied to the high priest in the LXX, nor even to blemishless sacrificial animals,[91] but it was in Philo to describe the sinlessness of the high priest (*Fug.* 118; *Spec.* I 113). By being sinless Christ fulfills not a condition of the priesthood according to the O.T., but a condition of the high priesthood according to Philo.

The writer notes other differences which set Christ higher than his O.T. types. The priests prior to Christ offered frequent and

---

[88] So G. Schrenk, TWNT III, p. 280 n. 61.

[89] See Lev. 4.2; 5.15; Num. 15.22–31. Judaism afterward maintained the distinction; see G. F. Moore, *op. cit.* I, pp. 463ff., and Heb. 10.26.

[90] See above p. 62.

[91] See E. Hatch, H. Redpath, *A Concordance to the Septuagint*, Oxford, 1897.

even daily sacrifices which were unable to take away sins (10.11; 5.3). But unlike them Christ does not need to sacrifice first for himself, and then for the people; his sacrifice is "once for all" (7.27), made not with animal blood but with his own blood (9.12, 25), and his one sacrifice does take away sins (10.14). The former priests were mortal; hence they could not long continue as priests. But Christ is immortal and therefore has the priesthood forever (7.23–25). The priests entered into a copy of the heavenly sanctuary, but Christ entered heaven itself (9. 24). They became priests without an oath; but Christ was sworn in as priest by God (7.20f., 28).

A more exact type of Christ is the priest Melchizedek, King of Salem (Gen. 14.17–20). Heb. builds a typology of Melchizedek of Christ as well as a typology of the O.T. priesthood in general because Psalm 110 contains the words, "The Lord has sworn, and will not change his mind. 'Thou art a priest forever after the order of Melchizedek' " (v. 4; 5.6, 10; 6.20; 7.11, 15, 17, 21). $\tau \dot{\alpha} \xi \iota \varsigma$ in this text was clearly understood by the writer to mean a "priestly order." [92] But he paraphrases the expression, "if another priest arises according to the likeness ($\varkappa \alpha \tau \dot{\alpha} \ \tau \dot{\eta} \nu \ \dot{\delta} \mu o \iota \dot{\delta} \tau \eta \tau \alpha$) of Melchizedek" (7.15). Similarly he says Melchizedek resembled ($\dot{\alpha} \varphi \omega \mu o \iota \omega \mu \dot{\epsilon} \nu o \varsigma$) the Son of God (7.3). Since Christ does not descend from a priestly order as the Levitical priests do (7.14–16), Heb. interprets the $\tau \dot{\alpha} \xi \iota \varsigma$ of Melchizedek as one of "likeness in kind" rather than priestly lineage. To explain the likeness of Melchizedek of Christ Heb. presents a *midrash* on Ps. 110.4 (chap. 7).

Heb.'s and Philo's picture of Melchizedek have one or two points in common. The name "Melchizedek" is etymologized by both writers in the same way, "King of Righteousness" and the title "King of Salem," "King of peace" as well (7.2; *LA* III 79). But here the similarity ends. In *LA* III 82 and *Cong.* 98f. Melchizedek is allegorized as human reason which rises in divine intoxication to God. Since the etymologies are natural ones we need assume no contact whatever between the two interpretations of Melchizedek. Nor does there seem to be any affinity between the

---

[92] So he speaks of Christ being a priest "not $\varkappa \alpha \tau \dot{\alpha} \ \tau \dot{\eta} \nu \ \tau \dot{\alpha} \xi \iota \nu$ of Aaron" (7.11). The papyri know the use of $\tau \dot{\alpha} \xi \iota \varsigma$ meaning a priestly office; see J. Moulton-G. Milligan, *op. cit.*; U. Wilcken-L. Mittels, *Grundzüge und Chrestomathie der Papyruskunde*, Leipzig-Berlin, 1912, I/II, 80.16.

picture of Melchizedek in Heb. and that found in any extant Jewish interpretations.[93]

Heb.'s exegesis of Ps. 110.4 is remarkable to say the least. In the phrase "thou art a priest forever after the order of Melchizedek" the writer relates the word "forever" both to Christ and to Melchizedek. Unlike mortal priests Melchizedek "lives" (7.8), and "having neither beginning of days nor end of life . . . he remains a priest forever" (7.3). Christ's "likeness" of Melchizedek is that he becomes a priest "according to the power of an indestructible life," that is, like the indestructible life of Melchizedek (7.15–17).

It was the second rule of the *middoth* of Rabbi Hillel, called *gezerah shawah*, that if two separate passages of scripture contained the same word, the two texts belonged together and ex-

---

[93] E. Käsemann, *op. cit.*, p. 130, thinks there is a Gnostic-Jewish speculation reflected here in which Melchizedek was the *Urmensch* incarnation which began with Adam and was repeatedly incarnated in generations afterward until Melchizedek. After citing certain passages assembled by F.J. Jérôme, *Das geschichtliche Melchisedech-Bild und seine Bedeutung im Hebräerbriefe*, Strasbourg, 1920, pp. 10–17, Käsemann says (p. 131), "The striking parallel of these late-Jewish sources to the Christology of Hebrews cannot be denied." Actually, the only Jewish sources cited by Jérôme or Käsemann are the fragments from the *Slavonic Book of the Secrets of Enoch*, and the *Apocalypse of Abraham* (both re-worked by Christians). The references of Käsemann to these works just show that Melchizedek was buried in the earth, and that he was regarded as a great high priest. The connection Käsemann adduces between Melchizedek and Adam comes from a Christian Adam book which Jérôme admits may not even contain Jewish sources (p. 13). At any rate Jerome himself produced no specific parallel from this text to the interpretation of Melchizedek in Heb. In the only Gnostic text cited by Käsemann, *Pistis Sophia*, Melchizedek appears as the messenger of light who leads the purified souls to the source of light. Such a role has, of course, nothing in common with Melchizedek in Heb.

The later Christian group called the Melchizedekites betray no Gnostic character. Historically they belong to the Christian heresy Monarchianism. Their interest in Melchizedek was prompted by Heb., and they sought to show on the basis of Heb. that Melchizedek was higher than Christ, indeed that he was the God and father of Jesus Christ, or at any rate a higher power of God than Christ. See H. Stork, *Die sogenannten Melchisedekianer*, Leipzig, 1928, pp. 12, 26f., 68, 76–81; similarly G. Wuttke, *Melchisedech der Priesterkönig von Salem*, Giessen, 1927, p. 12 n. 12 n. 4. The lack of a polemic in Heb. against an over-estimate of Melchizedek like that against the high priest seems to indicate the writer had no Melchizedek veneration in mind as he was writing.

plained each other.[94] This principle of exegesis can be seen in Philo as well.[95] Heb. also employs this method of exposition. Finding the name "Melchizedek" in Ps. 110.4 the writer goes to Gen. 14.17–20 to define Melchizedek's priesthood as opposed to that of the Levitical priests (7.1–14). In the episode of Abraham's encounter with Melchizedek two things stand out in the writer's mind, both of which he sees relating to Melchizedek's priesthood. First, Melchizedek blessed Abraham (7.1) who had been entrusted with God's promises (7.6). This act in itself proved Melchizedek's superiority over all the descendents of Abraham, including the Levitical priests (7.5), for "It is beyond dispute that the inferior is blessed by the superior" (7.7). The connection with the Levitical priests in this thought concerning descendents becomes clearer in what the writer says about the tithe Abraham paid Melchizedek. A similar thought that the one who receives tithes is greater than the one who pays them is in the writer's mind, although he admits that the Levitical priests receive the tithe at the hands of their kinsmen of common descent from the patriarch Abraham (7.5). The fact that Abraham tithed to Melchizedek proves the superiority of Melchizedek's priesthood over the Levitical one:

> One might even say that Levi himself, who receives tithes, paid tithes through Abraham, for he was still in the loins of his ancestor when Melchizedek met him (7.9f.).

---

[94] For instance, *M^ekhiltha* at Ex. 21.27, *lahaphshii y^eshallhenu* ("he shall set him free"). R. Eliezer reasons this means a letter of dismissal is to be given to him: The verb *shalah* appears in Deut. 24.1. Since it involves a letter of dismissal there, such must be meant here; see H. Strack, *Einleitung in Talmud und Midraŝ*, Munich, 1921, p. 97, for other examples as well. J.W. Doeve, *Jewish Hermeneutics in the Synoptic Gospels and Acts*, Leiden, 1953, pp. 107–109, cites an illustration of this principle in Jam. 2.21–24. There the writer brings together Gen. 22.9 and Is. 41.8 with Gen. 15.6 in order to prove that Abraham's work of offering his son Isaac belonged to his justification. The three texts were collated to explain each other because all three contained a reference to "the seed of Abraham" (Gen. 15.5; 22.16, 17a; Is. 41.8).

[95] Citing Gen. 3.1, "Now the serpent was the most subtle of all the beasts on the earth, which the Lord God had made," Philo explains the significance of the passage by quoting Num. 21.6, Deut. 8.15f., Ex. 4.1f., Gen. 44.16–18 (*LA* II 71–94), all of which belong together because they contain the word "serpent". Similarly Gen. 16.2 and 28.7 are brought together because they both contain the verb "to hear" (*Cong.* 69f.).

Heb.'s decision that Melchizedek is "without father or mother or genealogy" (7.3) turns on the understanding that ordinarily one becomes a priest by family descent so that for the Levites genealogy was the first qualification for priesthood. The oddity of Melchizedek was that he was one priest without a genealogy, for scripture (Gen. 14.17–20) lists none for him as it otherwise does for priests. Such reasoning is an example of the argument from silence, *quod non in Thora non in mundo*, encountered in rabbinic exegesis [96] as well as in Philo. [97]

A glance at the N.T. shows that its writers interpreted the O.T. through Jesus Christ. But what is not always noted is that Christ was also interpreted through the O.T. [98] The O.T. types of Christ in Heb. are an indication that however much of Hellenism may be found in and behind the writer's argument, the thought always reverts to Biblical passages and persons that are used to describe and define the work and person of Christ.

---

[96] See Strack-Billerbeck, also O. Michel, *Paulus und seine Bibel*, p. 94f. Michel notes Paul's argument from the silence of Ps. 32.1 which says nothing about works, therefore they bring no blessedness (Rom. 4.6–8).

[97] Concerning Cain Philo says, "On no occasion did he meet with death. For nowhere in the Book of the Law has his death been mentioned" (*Det.* 178; cf. *Praem.* 68–70; *Virt.* 200; *Fug.* 60; *Conf.* 12). See for further examples from Philo, C. Büchel, *Der Hebräerbrief und das Alte Testament*, TSK, 1906, p. 575f.

[98] This is recognized in Heb. by S. Amsler, *L'Ancien Testament dans l'Église*, Neuchâtel, 1960, p. 25.

CHAPTER VIII

The Parenetic Typology

1: The Parenesis of the Lesser to the Greater

One of Rabbi Hillel's seven *middoth*, or rules of hermeneutics for the Torah, was the argument *a minori ad maius*, the principle *qal waḥomer*, "light and heavy."[1] According to this principle one reasons from the fullest conditions described in a legislation down to the lesser ones which are implicitly included in it, or from the lesser to the fuller conditions. The presupposition is that the Law is strictest in matters of weightiest importance, while laxer in things lighter. Thus, if one finds certain stipulations for a matter of lesser consequence, one can reason that the same principle would apply all the more in a similar case of much greater moment, even though the Torah laid down no specific rule in the matter.

Occasionally juridical arguments of the *a minori ad maius* kind are encountered in the N.T. (Lk. 13.15f.; 14.3–5; Mt. 12.11f.; Jn. 7.22f.), and the idea of *qal waḥomer* is translated by πόσῳ μᾶλλον or πολλῷ μᾶλλον.[2] Philo knows and uses the principle,[3] and terms it "forbidding from afar" (μακρόθεν or πόρρωθεν, *Spec.* III 48, 63, 117; IV 104; *Virt.* 137).[4] It is not certain whether in Philo this principle comes from the rabbis or Hellenism.[5]

---

[1] Hillel was not the originator of any of the *middoth;* he rather collated what at his time were hermeneutical rules in general use. See H. Strack, *Einleitung in Talmud und Midraŝ*, p. 96f.

[2] O. Michel, *Paulus und seine Bibel*, p. 92; F. Maas, "Von den Ursprüngen der rabbinischen Schriftauslegung," ZTK, 1955, p. 140f.; cf. Mt. 6.30; 7.11; 2 Cor. 3.8, 9, 11; Rom. 11.12, 24.

[3] For instance: "For if those who have reviled mortal parents are led away for execution (Ex. 21.15f.), what penalty must we consider that those have merited who take upon them to blaspheme the Father and Maker of the universe ?" (*Fug.* 84)

[4] See above p. 49f.

[5] D. Daube, "Rabbinic Methods of Interpretation and Hellenistic Rhetoric," HUCA, 1949, feels that the *qal waḥomer* concept was taken by the

Because in Heb. the two covenants are seen in typological relationship, O.T. instructions made to the people of the old covenant can be applied to the people of the new covenant in a "lesser to the greater," "how-much-more" parenesis. The reasoning is, if such things had validity under the old covenant represented as the "lighter" (*qal*) situation, how much more must they be true in the new covenant, seen as the "heavy" (*homer*) case. According to Heb.'s interpretation the blood of goats and bulls and the ashes of a heifer required under the Law sanctified one externally. "How much more" (πόσῳ μᾶλλον), then, can one expect the blood of Christ under the new covenant to cleanse one's conscience from the works of death (9.13f.). This conclusion is consistent with the theology of the whole letter which sees the new covenant (the *homer*) not only having more importance than the old (the *qal*), but becoming farther reaching in scope. In this aspect 9.13f. compares with Philo's reasoning from the prohibition (Lev. 22.28) against sacrificing a mother and infant on the same day to outlawing sacrificing any pregnant animals, finally to proscribing executing pregnant women (*Virt.* 134–139).

Following this thought, Heb. finds a typological parenesis for the Church in the punishments inflicted under the old covenant for disobedience. If every transgression of the Law spoken by angels was justly punished, how then shall we escape retribution if we neglect the salvation spoken by the Lord himself and confirmed to us by the apostles as well as divine miracles? (2.2–4) The writer evidently had Deut. 17.6 in mind, the provision for penalty of infractions against the covenant. Alluding to the passage later he gives it the same "lesser to the greater" treatment:

A man who has violated the law of Moses dies without mercy at the testimony of two or three witnesses. How much worse punishment do you think will be deserved by the man who has spurned the Son of God? (10.28)

rabbis from Hellenistic jurisprudence where it was also observed. I. Heinemann, *Philos jüdische und griechische Bildung*, p. 493 n. 6, gives several examples from Greek writers. Nevertheless, Philo's *a minori ad maius* conclusions occasionally show apparent acquaintance with rabbinic teaching. S. Belkin, *Philo and the Oral Law*, p. 32, parallels the conclusion reached by this argument from Num. 27.5–11, that the father may inherit the property of his child (*Spec.* II 132), with the same deduction in *Sifre Num.* 134.

Heb. recalls the experience of Israel's receiving the revelation on Mt. Sinai and admonishes the Church not to refuse Christ's word of revelation, τὸν λαλοῦντα (12.25).[6] If the people of Israel did not escape when they transgressed the word of revelation spoken on earth through Moses, much less (πολὺ μᾶλλον) shall we be able to escape punishment if we reject Christ who speaks to us from heaven.[7]

The doctrine of the impossibility of a second repentance after intentional (ἑκουσίως) sinning (10.26; 6.4–8) apparently rests upon a *qal waḥomer* deduction from Num. 15.27–31, where the distinction appears between an unintentional sin (ἀκούσια) which may be atoned, and sin "with a high hand," i.e., intentional sin, which may not be. So the writer has reasoned in 10.26 that if intentional sins were unforgivable under the old covenant, how much more unforgivable must be a believer's willful renunciation of Christ under the new covenant (v. 29).[8]

2: Parenetic Examples

In the above application of O.T. instructions the last four were interpreted so as to warn against apostasy, showing what the consequences of such unfaithfulness under the old covenant were. A couple of O.T. types of apostates are introduced as examples of the consequences of unfaithfulness. Heb. warns lest anyone

... be immoral or irreligious like Esau, who sold his birthright for a single meal. For you know that afterward, when he desired to inherit the blessing,

---

[6] On λαλέω for the communication of a divine revelation, see above p. 77 n. 9.

[7] It seems to me the writer is thinking of the setting in Ex. 19.10ff. In the immediate context preceding he has made two quotations from Ex. 19 (12.18, 20). The items mentioned in vv. 22–24 serve to emphasize the heavenly character of the new revelation as opposed to the earthly character of the previous one at Sinai. The contrast in v. 25 is still between the revealer on earth and the one *from* (ἀπὸ) heaven. The speaker on earth would be Moses (cf. λαλέω in Ex. 19.19; 20.19) whom the people would hear but not God (20.19), and the one from heaven is, of course, Christ. The people's refusing the one speaking on earth seems to be a general statement concerning any disobedience of Moses' words; so Moffatt.

[8] H. Kosmala, *op. cit.*, p. 120, notes the connection here with Num. 15. 27–31.

he was rejected, for he found no chance to repent, though he sought it with tears (12.16f.).

That Esau was licentious (πόρνος) was held by the rabbis,[9] but it was Philo's opinion as well (*Virt.* 208; *QG* IV 201; *LA* III 2; *Sac.* 81; *Mig.* 208). Here Esau is introduced as a type of one denied a second repentance, a point which accords with Heb.'s exegetical conclusions in 6.4–8; 10.26–28. The relevance of the illustration in view of the problem of apostasy is obvious.

The notion is much the same which is the basis for the type (4.11) of the Israelites in the wilderness spoken of in Ps. 95. Heb.'s reason for citing Ps. 95 (3.7–11, 15; 4.3, 5, 7) is not because he wishes to build a central theme around the motif of "the wandering people of God" exemplified in Israel in the wilderness.[10] After expounding on the psalm the writer expressly declares what the point of the text is, warning the Church to strive toward the rest of God and not to fall into the disobedience of which the Israelites in their apostasy in the wilderness are a type, a ὑπόδειγμα.[11] Paul also notes the Israelites were baptized into Moses in the cloud and sea, ate manna, and nevertheless were overthrown in the wilderness because they were unpleasing to God: "Now these things are types for us, not to desire evil as they did" (1 Cor. 10.6). According to Heb.'s interpretation Israel under Moses failed to enter the rest because the people sinned, disobeyed, and were unfaithful (3.16 to 19). Such is the apostasy the writer tells the Church to beware of (3.12).[12]

However Heb. finds a consolation for the Church in Ps. 95 as well. The writer thought the psalm was directed to the Church living in the new time of salvation. He finds this expressed in the opening word "today," indicating that God has fixed another season for offering the opportunity of entering his rest (4.7). Through David God has spoken of another day (4.8), the "today"

---

[9] See Strack-Billerbeck.

[10] As Käsemann, *op. cit.*, pp. 5–8, 12.

[11] See above p. 96f.

[12] A. Oepke, *op. cit.*, pp. 58–74, agrees with Käsemann that the motif in Heb., "the people of God," is a basic theme of the letter, but questions his assertion that the theme is necessarily the *wandering* people of God. He argues rightly that the point in 3.7–4.13 centered around Ps. 95 is rather a warning against apostasy.

in which the Church lives (3.13).[13] From the following phrase, "if you will hear his voice . . . ," Heb. concludes that because unbelief, refusal to hear God's voice, was denied admittance to the rest of God (Canaan) at the time of Joshua (Ps. 95.11; Heb. 4.8), "today" if the opposite occurs, namely belief, that will be rewarded by "a sabbath rest for the people of God" (4.2f., 9). Israel in the wilderness was offered the promise of entering God's rest if it believed; but since it did not believe, an unfulfilled promise of God in effect still remains to be fulfilled for those who will believe (4.1, 6).

Like Paul and Barnabas, who saw instances of the Gospel preached typologically in the O.T.,[14] Heb. interprets God's promise of entering his rest as a proclamation of the Gospel ($\varepsilon\dot{v}a\gamma\gamma\varepsilon\lambda i\zeta\varepsilon\sigma\vartheta a\iota$, 4.2, 6) made to Israel as well as to the Church. The writer never states explicitly what he understands by the psalm's mention of "the rest of God." But he applies the hermeneutical principle we observed earlier called *gezerah shawah*, according to which where the same term is mentioned in two different passages of Scripture, those passages belong together.[15] Thus he cites Gen. 2.2, "And God rested ($\varkappa a\tau\dot{\varepsilon}\pi a v\sigma\varepsilon v$) . . . from all his works" (4.4) immediately after citing Ps. 95.11 which mentions God's entering into his $\varkappa a\tau\dot{a}\pi a v\sigma\iota\varsigma$ (4.3), and therefore reasons that as one enters God's rest he would rest from his labors as God did from his (4.10). This alone does not explain what is meant by the "rest of God." But it is clear that the writer has taken the message of the psalm to be a promise of entering God's rest, which promise he identifies with the Gospel.[16] Elsewhere in the epistle the divine promises usually relate to future reward.[17] So the rest of God in Ps. 95

---

[13] This interpretation of "today" in Scripture as another season of time in which the people of God live is the opposite of its exposition in Philo where "today" is "the limitless age that never comes to an end" (*Fug.* 57; cf. *LA* III 25).

[14] Gal. 3.8; *Barn.* 9.7–9.

[15] See above p. 146.

[16] Cf. 4.1f.; J. Schniewind and G. Friedrich, TWNT II, p. 581 n. 67; Moffatt, Riggenbach, Windisch, and Michel.

[17] While the promises are not necessarily still to be fulfilled in 6.12 and 11.33 they otherwise await fulfillment: the scores of offspring promised (Gen. 15.5) were never seen by Abraham and Sarah (11.11f.; 6.12–15; 7.6); Abel, Enoch, Noah, Abraham, and Sarah, and the rest listed in Heb. 11 (cf. v. 39) never saw the fulfillment of the divine promises (11.13); the promised eternal inher-

must be a futuristic promise, an eschatological salvation whose type is the not yet fulfilled promise of entering the rest spoken of in the Pentateuch and psalm. This agrees with the late Jewish and early Christian usage which proclaimed an eschatological rest as a reward at the end time.[18]

3: Chapter Eleven

This chapter merits special consideration by itself in our study. The use of the O.T. here does not correspond to the rabbinic practices of "stringing pearls," that is, the citation of Scripture passages all on a given theme or point from different witnesses in the Law, prophets, and the writings.[19] Rather its use of Scripture follows the pattern identified by H. Thyen as "the Jewish Hellenistic Homily."[20] This homily often choose a theme, such as "repentance" in 1 Clem. 7.5ff., or "faith" in Heb. 11, and then selected a series of persons out of the O.T. who by their acts illustrated this idea.[21] Among the Hellenistic Jews Philo uses this device.[22]

---

itance awaits the new age (9.15); the better promises upon which the new covenant is based are not defined (8.6), but are probably God's words spoken for the future in Jer. 31 (8.8); see Schniewind-Friedrich, *ibid.*, p. 580f.

[18] 4 *Es.* 8.52; Rev. 14.13; *Barn.* 15.3–9; see Strack-Billerbeck, and Windisch at Heb. 4.3. G. von Rad's statement, "Allerdings ganz neu ist das Verständnis der Ruhe als eines jenseitigen Heilsgutes dessen die Gläubigen erst nach diesem Leben teilhaftig werden dürfen," in "Es ist noch eine Ruhe vorhanden dem Volke Gottes," *Zwischen den Zeiten*, 1933, p. 109, is true for this reinterpretation of the term "rest of God" within the Bible, but perhaps not for Jewish and Christian eschatology antedating Heb. The meaning given to the rest of God here and to God's resting in Gen. 2.2 is eschatological and not philosophical as in Philo for whom "God's rest is rather a working with absolute ease, without toil and without suffering" (*Cher.* 87; cf. *Sac.* 40).

[19] An example of this appears in Rom. 15.9–12, containing passages from all three on the theme of the Gentiles' glorifying God; see O. Michel, *Paulus und seine Bibel*, p. 84. K. Stendahl, *op. cit.*, p. 216, notes there are no such examples in the Gospels.

[20] *Op. cit.*, p. 16ff.

[21] *Ibid.*, pp. 76; 111–115. Thyen also cites as examples of this, 1 *Clem.* 4.1ff. on "jealousy," 9.2ff. on "obedience and faithfulness," 4 *Macc.* 2, 3 on "reason," and *Wisd.* 10 on the deliverance of Wisdom.

[22] Cf. his homily on nobility, *Virt.* 198–227, on being added or translated, *Sac.* 5–7, on prophecy, *Her.* 260–262, and on being naked before God, *LA* II 57–59.

The subjects for study chosen by Heb. are listed under the heading "faith," although the texts referred to practically never mention this characteristic in their treatments of the persons the writer feels exemplify this quality.[23] These Biblical examples are brought forth parenetically to illustrate faith as (1) trusting in God who is invisible (11.3, 6, 27), and (2) trusting in God's promises made for the future.[24] 11.1 is a very general statement about faith, not a definition of faith in God[25] for God is not even mentioned in it. But the first of the above-mentioned characteristics of faith is implied in 11.1b, "things not seen," and the second in 11.1a, "things hoped for."[26]

Because of its affinity in form with numerous Jewish meditations of the same kind, and because there is nothing in the chapter except v. 26 and 39f. which a Jew could not have written just as well, several scholars have thought the writer took up a Jewish homily and re-worked it, fitting it into his argument.[27] However, the section's vocabulary as well as the style show affinity with the rest of the letter,[28] so if the writer had such a prototype before him when he wrote the chapter, at any rate he must have thoroughly re-written it in his own vocabulary from his own theological concern. But whether the writer was referring to a specific document while writing chapter 11 or not, it is at any rate clear that much of the exegetical material comes from Jewish Alexandrian school tradition witnessed to as well in Philo.

The author states the world, created by the Word of God, "came into being, the seen from the unseen ($\mu\grave{\eta}$ $\grave{\epsilon}\varkappa$ $\varphi\alpha\iota\nu o\mu\acute{\epsilon}\nu\omega\nu$, v. 3), and thereby implies that the world of sense is $\tau\grave{\alpha}$ $\varphi\alpha\iota\nu\acute{o}\mu\epsilon\nu\alpha$, a frequent designation of Philo for the phenomenal world (*Opif.* 45; *Agr.* 42;

---

[23] In his commentary Windisch (p. 98) recalls that the only passage mentioning "faith" in connection with the episodes described in Heb. 11, Gen. 15.6, is never alluded to in the chapter.

[24] Cf. especially 11.6, 7–11, 13a, 26b, 39; see on these two aspects of faith Barrett, *op. cit.*, p. 381.

[25] So Riggenbach, Westcott, Michel.

[26] See R. Bultmann, TWNT VI, p. 207f.

[27] So Windisch, Michel, Héring, H. Thyen, *op. cit.*, p. 18, and E. Stauffer, *Die Theologie des Neuen Testaments*, Stuttgart, 1941, p. 217f.

[28] See L. Blass, "Die rhythmische Komposition des Hebräerbriefes, TSK, 1902, pp. 420–461. Even Thyen grants chapter 11 is composed in the writer's words.

ὁ φαινόμενος κόσμος, *Mig.* 105, 179; τὸ φαινόμενον *Conf.* 172). In *Conf.* 172 Philo says that through the divine powers,

> the incorporeal and intelligible world was framed, the archetype of this phenomenal world (τοῦ φαινομένου), that being a system of invisible ideal forms, as this is of visible material bodies.

In saying that the visible world has come into being out of the non-phenomenal world, Heb. does not necessarily think that it was structured through the invisible ideas, as in Philo's Platonism.[29] But a term from Philo's Genesis commentary nevertheless recurs in Heb.'s reference to Gen. 1.

Gen. 4.10 states that Abel's blood cried out from the ground (cf. Heb. 12.24), but when Heb. says that though he died through his sacrifice "he is still speaking" (v. 4), the writer touches upon a tradition known to him and Philo who explains that Abel is both dead and alive: "Abel, therefore, strange as it seems, has both been put to death and lives: he is destroyed or abolished out of the mind of the fool (Abel), but he is alive with the happy life in God," for, Philo asks, "how could one no longer existing speak?" (*Det.* 48; cf. 70)

Heb.'s claim (v. 10) that Abraham was seeking a city whose builder was God has already been traced to Alexandrian exegesis.[30] It is strange that no commentator has attempted to explain the problematic v. 11 from Philo's writings. The writer says, "By faith Sarah herself received power to conceive;" but the idiom καταβολὴ σπέρματος which he uses was always a term for the male function in begetting offspring and never intended the conception of the female.[31] This difficulty has caused Michel, Riggenbach, and others to think "Sarah herself" should be read as a dative rather than nominative, αὐτῇ Σάρρᾳ, making the subject Abraham

---

[29] As Windisch. The phrase perhaps should be translated, "out of that *not yet* manifest." For μὴ as the negative of what has not yet happened, see A. Robertson, *A Grammer of the Greek New Testament in the Light of Historical Research*, Nashville, 1934, p. 1167. More is not especially intended than the words, "I commanded . . . that visible things should come from invisible," and "I tell to thee . . . all that I created from non-being, and visible things from invisible" (*Secrets of Enoch* 25.1; 24.2).

[30] See above p. 72f.

[31] The Greek fathers were puzzled over this and offered various explanations; see Westcott, Riggenbach, and Spicq. Philo illustrates the proper use of καταβάλλω σπέρμα in *Ebr.* 211, *Sob.* 36; *Opif.* 132; *Cong.* 131; *Cher.* 49.

"with Sarah herself." But the passage becomes clear when we remember that in Philo's allegory Sarah consistently represents Virtue,[32] synonymous with Sophia, which brings the heavenly learning to Abraham (*LA* II 82; *Cher.* 9; *Cong.* 22f.). Therefore Philo says that in the case of Abraham and Sarah, it is the female, Virtue, who sows the seeds of correct instruction in the wise man, Abraham:

> Now in a marriage where the union is brought about by pleasure, the partnership is between body and body, but in the marriage made by wisdom [Sarah] it is between thoughts which seek purification and perfect virtues... For in the bodily marriage the male sows the seed and the female receives it; on the other hand in the matings within the soul, though virtue seemingly ranks as wife, her natural function is to sow good counsels and excellent words to inculcate tenets truly profitable to life, while thought, though held to take the place of the husband, receives the holy and divine sowings.[33] (*Abr.* 100f.; cf. *Fug.* 51f.)

As it stands, Heb. 11.11 is, of course, no allegory like that proposed by Philo. But if we think of the writer as knowing the Alexandrian allegory by which Sarah, Virtue or Sophia, paradoxically sows seeds of learning, we can readily understand why a phrase like $\varkappa\alpha\tau\alpha\beta o\lambda\grave{\eta}$ $\sigma\pi\acute{e}\rho\mu\alpha$, associated in his mind with the figure Sarah, has slipped into his homily as he recalls Sarah's miraculous conception.

Heb.'s conclusion that all the foregoing people (Abel, Enoch, Noah, Abraham, and Sarah) were "strangers and exiles upon the earth" (v. 13) recalls similar phrases in Gen. 23.4, 1 Chr. 29.15, and Ps. 39.13, but is a generalization made nowhere in the O.T. But Philo says that Scripture's wise men are all

> represented as sojourners ... to them the heavenly region, where their citizenship lies, is their native land; the earthly region in which they became sojourners is a foreign country (*Conf.* 77f.).

---

[32] *Cher.* 3–10; *Cong.* 1–13; *Mut.* 61, 77–80, and other passages listed in Loeb's edition, Vol. X, p. 413 n. a.

[33] E. Goodenough, *By Light, Light*, p. 23, links Philo's Sophia with the begetting quality to various Hellenistic mystery female deities who had similar functions. The seeds of Virtue according to Stoic thought are a more likely source for the idea. Stoicism thought that Nature sowed the good seed of Virtue into a person, but this is overgrown by weeds. It is teachable, but only after reason becomes free of false opinion can it be called *orthos logos*. See M. Pohlenz, *Die Stoa*, I p. 124.

This parallel is also illuminating in view of Heb.'s judgment that the heroes of faith sought a fatherland (v. 14), "that is, a heavenly one" (v. 16). Philo also says all generated beings

> enjoy equal honour and equal rights, but to God they are aliens and so-journers. For each of us has come into this world as into a foreign city . . . and in this city he does but sojourn, until he has exhausted his appointed span of life (*Cher*. 120).

By mentioning "God has prepared for them a city" (v. 16), Heb. emphasizes the same motif, for "in reality a wise man's soul ever finds heaven to be his fatherland and earth a foreign country . . . and looks on himself as a stranger and sojourner in it" (*Agr*. 65; cf. *Conf*. 80f; *Som*. I 181; *QG* III 10).

Merely on the basis of his rescuing a Hebrew (Ex. 2.11f.), Moses is said to have refused to be regarded as son of Pharaoh's daughter, reckoning "the abuse of Christ" greater reward than Egypt's treasures (vv. 24–26). This Moses legend is attested to by Philo:

> He gave up the lordship of Egypt, which he held as son to the daughter of the then reigning king, because the sight of the inquities committed in the land and his own nobility of soul and magnanimity of spirit and inborn hatred of evil led him to renounce completely his expected inheritance from the kinsfolk of his adoption (*Mos*. I 149; cf. 32).

One feature distinctive from Philo in chap. 11, however, is the referring to Biblical material outside the Torah in vv. 30–40. Philo seldom cites Scripture outside the Pentateuch, and there is reason to believe that his canon of Scripture extended no farther than the Torah.[34] Contrasted with Philo who believed Judaism made no progress after Moses,[35] Heb. combines the Pentateuch material with that from the prophets and intertestamental literature into one *Heilsgeschichte* extending down to the time of our own salvation (v. 40).

---

[34] Goodenough, *ibid*., p. 75f.
[35] *Ibid*.

Conclusion

This study has underscored the lack of allegory in Heb. as it was defined and used by the allegorists. The absence of this hermeneutical tool is particularly conspicuous because of the Alexandrian background of the epistle. Because allegory was the outstanding exegetical principle practiced in Alexandrian circles, its omission in Heb. also means that the writer has excluded Alexandrian hermeneutics *par excellence*. To be sure, certain exegetical practices are shared by Philo and Heb. But these are such devices as *qal wahomer*, *gezerah shawah*, and *quod non in Thora non in mundo* which appear in Rabbinic and other brands of Judaism as well, and even in other parts of the N.T.

Nevertheless the exegetical conclusions reached by the Alexandrian school of Jewish allegorists are firmly in the writer's mind, and the results of their work can frequently be seen behind his argument. At times, as in chap. 11, the writer merely says things in passing which betray his exposure to the school's tradition, notions frequently having been worked out through allegory but whose original arguments and bases have now been omitted. Such are remembrances, fossils of a now extinct creature.

In other instances recollections of allegorical apologies have affected Heb.'s anti-Judaic argument. Endeavors to show how the Law was eternal, a doctrine for the life of the soul, a shadow of deeper truths, all lie behind the writer's emphasizing how the Law was relative to a certain time, outdated externalism, having *only* a shadow of the real realities. Efforts to show why, as disclosed through the symbolic interpretation of the temple and high priest, Judaism was the universal religion for all mankind are apparent over against the minimizing of the earth-bound sanctuary and the priests who were sinners themselves and never ascended into the heavenly tabernacle. In this way Jewish allegorical apology was a

137

Vorgeschichte to Christian preaching as it is seen in Heb.[1] The *praeparatio evangelica* of the Alexandrian Jewish allegorists was that by selecting certain Biblical legislation and institutions for allegorical treatment which had been censured by Hellenistic thinkers, it thereby opened the way for early Christianity to steal the ark from Judaism's camp. With some modifications the writer of Heb. has brought up again the same objections against such institutions in Judaism made by various non-Jews which had given issue to their allegorization. In Heb. such are being disputed because they do not measure up to what their allegories claim for them.

The question naturally arises: Why did not the writer use the already familiar allegorical hermeneutics in his polemic against Judaism? Why did he not argue, as is done in the *Epistle of Barnabas*,[2] that the various types of Christ and the sacrificial victims of the O.T. *were* Christ according to the hidden meaning? The answer must be, because his theology of the two covenants, based on his understanding of *Heilsgeschichte*, in an adroit way has put the old and the new covenants in typological parallel without blurring their distinctions. For the cause of so changed a view of the Bible and its history as we find in Heb. compared with Philo we must look somewhere other than to the Jewish background of the letter. It must have been a result of the common thinking and faith of the whole body of Christ.

---

[1] And as M. Friedländer, *Geschichte der jüdischen Apologetik als Vorgeschichte des Christentums*, Zürich, 1903, tried to argue for various concepts in the N.T.

[2] See above p. 91 n. 6.

Appendix

A Note on Textual Alteration

K. Stendahl has studied the phenomenon of free O.T. citations in Matthew and the Biblical interpretation (*pesher*) of the Qumran *Habakkuk Commentary*, and has concluded that such loose citing is due to a kind of targumizing which was familiar with several textual readings, and chose the one best suited for the occasion, which type of study he calls the *midrash pesher*.[1] B. Gärtner[2] has shaken Stendahl's thesis, questioning whether an exegetical "school" with so many textual variations at its disposal as Stendahl asserts can be posited. Nevertheless the changing of Scripture quotations is one characteristic of the *pesher*, as opposed to the *midrashim* of the Tannaites,[3] which Stendahl's work has established.[4]

Among the non-Tannaites there was apparently some bit of textual alteration in commentary. It cannot, of course, be said with certainty that a writer has altered his Biblical manuscript simply because his reading varies from all manuscript evidence available to us, since there were countless readings that have not come down to us. Unless a writer quotes his MS one way, and then in his commentary deliberately changes it, we dare not say with certainty he has emended his text. But Philo does this very thing when he cites Gen. 4.8 first, "Cain rose up against Abel his brother and slew him," and then says, "It must be read in this way, 'Cain rose up and slew himself'" (*Det.* 47).

---

[1] *The School of St. Matthew*, Uppsala, 1954; see especially pp. 157–202.

[2] "The Habakkuk Commentary (DSH) and the Gospel of Matthew," *Studia Theologica*, 1954, pp. 1–24.

[3] J. Bonsirven, *Exégèse rabbinique et exégèse paulinienne*, Paris, 1939, pp. 335–337.

[4] Gärtner, *op. cit.*, p. 13.

Heb. has also altered Jer. 31.33f., citing it differently (10.16) than his MS (8.10, 12):

αὕτη ἡ διαθήκη ἣν διαθήσομαι τῷ οἴκῳ Ἰσραήλ
μετὰ τὰς ἡμέρας ἐκείνας, λέγει κύριος,
διδοὺς νόμους μου εἰς τὴν διάνοιαν αὐτῶν,
καὶ ἐπὶ καρδίας αὐτῶν ἐπιγράψω αὐτούς,
... καὶ τῶν ἁμαρτιῶν αὐτῶν οὐ μὴ μνησθῶ ἔτι. (8.10, 12)
αὕτη ἡ διαθήκη ἣν διαθήσομαι πρὸς αὐτούς
μετὰ τὰς ἡμέρας ἐκείνας, λεγει κύριος
διδοὺς νόμους μου ἐπὶ καρδίας αὐτῶν
καὶ ἐπὶ τὴν διάνοιαν αὐτῶν ἐπιγράψω αυτούς,
καὶ τῶν ἁμαντιῶν αὐτῶν καὶ τῶν ἀνομιῶν αὐτῶν
οὐ μὴ μνησθήσομαι ἔτι. (10.16)

T. W. Manson[5] explains that these changes and others like them[6] are because the early Jewish and Christian expositors probably did not know our sharp distinction between the objective text and the subjective interpretation of it. They had greater confidence than we do in their ability to find the meaning of the text which was of primary importance to them. Once the meaning was found the primary task for them was not to accurately reproduce the traditional wording of it, but to express its sense.

---

[5] "The Argument from Prophecy," *Journal of Theological Studies*, 1945, p. 135f.

[6] For instance the addition of πᾶς in Rom. 10.11 to Is. 28.16, omitted in 9.33.

Bibliography

Adlington, W., *Apuleius the Golden Ass*, revized by S. Gaselee, The Loeb Classical Library, London, 1935.

Allegro, J., "Further Messianic References in Qumran Literature," JBL, 1956.

Amsler, S., *L'Ancien Testament dans l'Église*, Neuchâtel, 1960.

Von Arnim, H., *Stoicorum Veterum Fragmenta* I–III, Leipzig, 1905f.

Barrett, C.K., "The Eschatology of the Epistle to the Hebrews," *The Background of the New Testament and its Eschatology*, Cambridge, 1956.

Barth, M., *Was Christ's Death a Sacrifice?*, Edinburgh, 1961.

Belkin, S., *Philo and the Oral Law*, Cambridge, Mass., 1942.

Bell, H., *Jews and Christians in Egypt, London*, 1924.

Bentzen, A., *Messias, Moses redivivus, Menschensohn*, Zurich, 1948.

Bietenhard, H., *Die himmlische Welt im Urchristentum und Spätjudentum*, Tübingen, 1951.

Billerbeck, P., Strack, H., *Kommentar zum Neuen Testament aus Talmud und Midrasch*, Munich, 1926ff.

Blass, L., "Die rhythmische Komposition des Hebräerbriefes," TSK, 1902.

Bolkestein, H., *Theophrastos Charakter der Deisidaimonia als religionsgeschichtliche Urkunde* (*Religionsgeschichtliche Versuche und Vorarbeiten* 21, Heft 2), Giessen, 1929.

Bonsirven, J., "Exégèse allégorique chez les rabbins tannaites," *Recherches de science religieuse*, 1933.

– *Exégèse rabbinique et exégèse paulinienne*, Paris, 1939.

– *St. Paul. Epître aux Hébreux*, Paris, 1943.

Bousset, W., "Die Lehre des Hermes Trismegistus," *Göttingische Gelehrte Anzeigen*, 1914.

– *Die Religion des Judentums im späthellenistischen Zeitalter*, third ed. by H. Gressmann, Tübingen, 1926.

Bornkamm, G., "Das Bekenntnis im Hebräerbrief," TB, 1942.

Box, H., *Philonis Alexandrini in Flaccum*, Oxford, 1939.

Bréhier, E., *Les idées philosophiques et religieuses de Philon d'Alexandrie*, Paris, 1908.

Bruce, F. F., *The Book of Acts*, London, 1951.

Bultmann, R., "Ursprung und Sinn der Typologie als hermeneutische Methode," TL, 1950.

Büchel, C., *Der Hebräerbrief und das Alte Testament*, TSK, 1906.

Büchsel, F., *Die Christologie des Hebräerbriefes*, Gütersloh, 1922.

141

Carmignac, J., "L'utilité ou l'inutilité des sacrifices sanglants dans la 'Règle de la Communauté' de Qumrân," RB, 1956.

Charles, R., *The Apocrypha and Pseudepigrapha of the Old Testament*, Vol. I–II, Oxford, 1913.

Cohn, L., Leisegang, H., Heinemann, I., *Die Werke Philos von Alexandria*, Vol. I–IV, Breslau, 1909–1938.

- Wendland, P., Reiter, S., *Philonis Alexandrini Opera quae supersunt*, Vol. I–VI and indices by H. Leisegang, 1896–1930, Berlin.

Colson, F., Whitaker, G., Earp, J., *Philo with an English Translation*, Vol. I–X with two supplements, The Loeb Classical Library, London, 1929 to 1962.

Cullmann, O., "The Significance of the Qumran Texts for Research into the Beginnings of Christianity," JBL, 1955.

- "A New Approach to the Interpretation of the Fourth Gospel," ET, 1959.

Dahl, N., "A New and Living Way," *Interpretation*, 1951.

Dalbert, P., *Die Theologie der hellenistischen jüdischen Missionsliteratur unter Ausschluss von Philo und Josephus* (*Theologische Forschungen*, Heft 4), Hamburg, 1954.

Daube, D., "Rabbinic Methods of Interpretation and Hellenistic Rhetoric," HUCA, 1949.

- "Alexandrian Methods of Interpretation and the Rabbis," *Festschrift Hans Lewald*, Basel, 1953.

Delling, G., "Wunder-Allegorie-Mythus bei Philon von Alexandreia," *Gottes ist der Orient, Festschrift für O. Eissfeldt*, Berlin, 1959.

Diels, H., *Fragmente der Vorsokratiker* I–III, Berlin, 1951.

Dodd, C.H., *The Bible and the Greeks*, London, 1935.

- *According to the Scriptures*, London, 1952.

- *The Interpretation of the Fourth Gospel*, Cambridge, 1953.

Eichrodt, W., "Ist die typologische Exegese sachgemässe Exegese?" TL, 1956.

- *Theologie des Alten Testaments* I⁶, Stuttgart, 1959.

Ellis, E.E., *Paul's Use of the Old Testament*, Edinburgh, 1957.

Eltester, F., *Eikon im Neuen Testament* (BZNW 24), Berlin, 1958.

Findlay, J.A., "The Book of Testimonies and the Structure of the First Gospel," *The Expositor*, 1920.

Friedländer, M., *Geschichte der jüdischen Apologetik als Vorgeschichte des Christentums*, Zurich, 1903.

Fritsch, C., *The Anti-Anthropomorphismus of the Greek Pentateuch*, Princeton, 1943.

Gärtner, B., "The Habakkuk Commentary (DSH) and the Gospel of Matthew," *Studia Theologica*, 1954.

Geiger, F., *Philon von Alexandreia als sozialer Denker* (*Tübinger Beiträge zur Altertumswissenschaft*, XVI), Stuttgart, 1932.

Gfrörer, A., *Philo und die Alexandrinische Theosophie* I, Stuttgart, 1831.

Goodenough, E., "Philo's Exposition of the Law and his De Vita Mosis," *The Harvard Theological Review*, 1933.

"A Neo-Pythagorean Source in Philo Judaeus," *Yale Classical Studies*, 1932.

142

- *By Light, Light*, New Haven, 1935.
- *Jewish Symbols in the Greco-Roman Period* IV, New York, 1954.

Goppelt, L., *Typos: Die typologische Deutung des Alten Testaments im Neuen*, Gütersloh, 1939.

Grant, R., *The Letter and the Spirit*, London, 1957.

Gressmann, H., *Der Messias*, Göttingen, 1929.

Grundmann, W., "Die Νήπιοι in der urchristlichen Paranese," NTS, 1959.

Hadas, M., *Aristeas to Philocrates*, New York, 1951.

Harder, F., "Die Septuagintazitate des Hebräerbriefes," *Theologia Viatorum*, Munich, 1939.

Harris, J.R., *Testimonies* I–II, London, 1916, 1920.

Hartwig, H., *Der Stil der jüdisch-hellenistischen Homilie*, Göttingen, 1955.

Hatch, E., Redpath, H., *A Concordance to the Septuagint*, Oxford, 1897.

Heinemann, I., "Die Lehre vom ungeschriebenen Gesetz," HUCA, 1927.
- *Philons griechische und jüdische Bildung*, Breslau, 1932.
- *Altjüdische Allegoristik*, Breslau, 1936.
- "Zur griechischen Allegoristik," *Mnemosyne*, 1949.
- "Die Allegoristik der hellenistischen Juden ausser Philon," *Mnemosyne*, 1952.

Héring, J., *L'Épître aux Hébreux*, Neuchâtel, 1955.

Hersman, R., *Studies in Greek Allegorical Interpretation*, Chicago, 1906.

Heyde, J.H., "Typus: Ein Beitrag zur Bedeutungsgeschichte des Wortes," *Forschungen und Fortschritte*, 1941.

Hirzel, R., ΑΓΡΑΘΟΣ ΝΟΜΟΧ (*Abhandlungen der sächsischen Gesellschaft, phil.-hist Klasse* xx), Leipzig, 1900.

Hühn, E., *Die alttestamentlichen Citate und Reminiscenzen im Neuen Testament*, Tübingen, 1900.

Hunt, B.P.W. Stather, *Primitive Gospel Sources*, New York, 1951.

Jérôme, F.J., *Das geschichtliche Melchisedech-Bild und seine Bedeutung im Hebräerbriefe*, Strasbourg, 1920.

Jülicher, A., *Die Gleichnisreden Jesu*[2] I, Leipzig, 1899.

Käsemann, E., *Das wandernde Gottesvolk*[2], Göttingen, 1957.

Kosmala, H., *Hebräer-Essener-Christen, Studien zur Vorgeschichte der frühchristlichen Verkündigung*, Leiden, 1959.

Kögel, J., "Der Begriff τελειοῦν im Hebräerbrief," *Theologische Studien Martin Kähler zum 6.Januar 1905 dargebracht*, Leipzig, 1905.

Kroll, W., *Procli Diadochi in Platonis rem publicam commentarii* II, Leipzig, 1901.

Kuhlmann, G., *Theologia Naturalis bei Philon und bei Paulus* (*Neutestamentliche Forschungen*, Heft 7), Gütersloh, 1930.

Kuhn, K.G., "The Two Messiahs of Aaron and Israel," *The Scrolls and the New Testament*, ed. K. Stendahl, New York, 1957.

Lampe, G.W.H., and Woolecombe, K.J., *Essays on Typology*, London, 1957.

Lauterbach, J., "The Ancient Jewish Allegorists in the Talmud and Midrash," *Jewish Quarterly Review*, 1910.

Leisegang, H., *Der Heilige Geist* I/I, Leipzig, 1919.
- *Indices ad Philonis Alexandrini Opera* I–II, Berlin, 1926–1930.

Leonard, W., *The Authorship of the Epistle to the Hebrews*, London, 1939.

Lewy, H., *Sobria Ebrietas* (ZNW Beih. 9), Giessen, 1929.

Lobue, F., "The Historical Background of the Epistle to the Hebrews," JBL, 1956.

Lohmeyer, E., *Diatheke. Ein Beitrag zur Erklärung des neutestamentlichen Begriffes*, Leipzig, 1913.

De Lubac, H., "'Typologie' et 'allegorisme,'" *Recherches de Science Religieuse*, 1947.

– *Histoire et esprit*, Paris, 1950.

Lundberg, Per, *La typologie baptismale dans l'ancienne Église*, Uppsala, 1942.

Mac Neill, H. L., *The Christology of the Epistle to the Hebrews*, Chicago, 1914.

Manson, T. W., "The Argument from Prophecy," *Journal of Theological Studies*, 1945.

– "The Problem of the Epistle to the Hebrews," *Bulletin of the John Rylands Library*, 1949.

Manson, W., *The Epistle to the Hebrews*, Edinburgh, 1951.

Maybaum, J., *Die Anthropomorphien und Anthropopathien bei Onkelos und den spätern Targumim mit besonderer Berücksichtigung der Ausdrücke Memra, Jᵉkara, und Schechintha*, Breslau, 1870.

Michel, O., *Paulus und seine Bibel*, Gütersloh, 1929.

– "Die Lehre von der christlichen Vollkommenheit nach der Anschauung des Hebräerbriefes," TSK, 1934–1935.

– *Der Brief an die Hebräer*,⁹ Göttingen, 1957.

Milligan, G., *The Theology of the Epistle to the Hebrews*, Edinburgh, 1899.

Moe, O., "Das Priestertum Christi im Neuen Testament ausserhalb des Hebräerbriefs," TL, 1947.

– "Das irdische und das himmlische Heiligtum," *Theologische Zeitschrift*, 1953.

Moffatt, J., *The Epistle to the Hebrews*, Edinburgh, 1924.

Moore, G. F., *Judaism in the First Centuries of the Christian Era* I–II, Cambridge, 1927.

Moulton, J., Milligen, G., *The Vocabulary of the Greek Testament*, London, 1928.

Mras, K., *Praeparatio Evangelica, Die griechischen christlichen Schriftsteller der ersten Jahrhunderte* III/I–II, Berlin, 1954–1956.

Nestle, W., *Vom Mythos zum Logos*, Stuttgart, 1940.

Oepke, A., *Das neue Gottesvolk*, Gütersloh, 1950.

Padva, P., *Les citations de l'Ancien Testament dans l'épître aux Hébreux*, Paris, 1904.

Paschar, J., *He Basilike Hodos. Der Königsweg zu Wiedergeburt und Vergöttung bei Philon von Alexandreia (Studien zur Geschichte und Kultur des Altertums)*, Paderborn, 1931.

Pépin, J., *Mythe et allégorie*, Paris, 1958.

Pierce, C. A., *Conscience in the New Testament*, London, 1955.

Van der Ploeg, J., "L'exégèse de l'Ancien Testament dans l'épître aux Hébreux," RB, 1947.

Plooij, D., *Studies in the Testimony Book*, Amsterdam, 1932.

Plutarch, *De Moralia*, The Loeb Classical Library, London, 1927 ff.

144

Pohlenz, M., *Die Stoa* I–II, Göttingen, 1948.

– , *Philon von Alexandreia* (*Nachrichten von der Akademie der Wissenschaften in Göttingen, phil.-hist. Kl. Nr. 5*), 1942.

Prigent, P., *Les testimonia dans le Christianisme primitif. L'épître de Barnabe*, Paris, 1962.

Von Rad, G., "Es ist noch eine Ruhe vorhanden dem Volke Gottes," *Zwischen den Zeiten*, 1933.

Reicke, B., *The Disobedient Spirits and Christian Baptism*, Lund, 1946.

Reitzenstein, R., *Poimandres, Studien zur griechisch-ägyptischen und frühchristlichen Literatur*, Leipzig, 1904.

– *Die hellenistischen Mysterienreligionen,*[3] Leipzig, 1927.

Riggenbach, E., *Der Brief an die Hebräer,*[2] Leipzig, 1922.

"Der Begriff τελείωσις im Hebräerbrief," *Neue kirchliche Zeitschrift*, 1923.

Robertson, A., *A Grammer of the Greek New Testament in the Light of Historical Research*, Nashville, 1934.

Rosenblatt, S., *The Interpretation of the Bible in the Mishnah*, Baltimore, 1935.

Ryle, H., *Philo and the Holy Scriptures*, London, 1895.

Sandmel, S., *Philo's Place in Judaism*, Cincinnati, 1956.

Schille, G., "Erwägungen zur Hohenpriesterlehre des Hebräerbriefes," ZNW, 1955.

Schwyzer, H.R., *Chairemon* (*Klassisch-philologische Studien* 4), Leipzig, 1932.

Scott, E.F., *The Epistle to the Hebrews: Its Doctrine and Significance*, Edinburgh, 1923.

Seeberg, A., *Der Brief an die Hebräer*, Leipzig, 1912.

– "Zur Auslegung von Heb. 2.5–18," *Neue Jahrbücher für deutsche Theologie*, 1894.

Selwyn, E., *The First Epistle of St. Peter*, London, 1946.

Shroyer, M., "Alexandrian Jewish Literalists," JBL, 1936.

Siegfried, C., *Philo von Alexandria als Ausleger des Alten Testaments*, Jena, 1875.

Simon, M., *St. Stephen and the Hellenists in the Primitive Church*, London, 1958.

Spicq, C., *L'épître aux Hébreux*, I–II, Paris, 1952.

– "L'origine johannique de la conception du Christ-prêtre dans l'épître aux Hébreux," in *Aux sources de la tradition chrétienne, Mélanges M. Goguel*, Neuchâtel, 1950.

Stauffer, E., *Die Theologie des Neuen Testaments*, Stuttgart, 1941.

Stein, E., *Die allegorische Exegese des Philo aus Alexandreia* (ZAW Beih. 51), 1929.

– *Philo und der Midrash* (ZAW Beih. 57), 1931.

– *Alttestamentliche Bibelkritik in der späthellenistischen Literatur*, Lwow, 1935.

Stendahl, K., *The School of St. Matthew*, Uppsala, 1954.

Stork, H., *Die sogenannten Melchisedekianer*, Leipzig, 1928.

Strack, H., *Einleitung in Talmud und Midras*, Munich, 1921.

Strathmann, H., *Der Brief an die Hebräer,*[5] Göttingen, 1949.

Tasker, R., *The Old Testament in the New Testament*, London, 1954.

Tate, J., "The Beginnings of Greek Allegory," CR, 1927.

– "Plato and Allegorical Interpretation," CQ, 1929.

– "On the History of Allegorism," *ibid.*

Thackeray, H. St. J., Marcus, R., *Josephus with an English Translation* I–VIII, The Loeb Classical Library, London, 1926 ff.

Turowski, E., *Die Widerspiegelung des stoischen Systems bei Philon von Alexandreia*, Borna, Leipzig, 1927.

Vaganay, L., "Le plan de l'épître aux Hébreux," in *Mémorial Lagrange*, Paris, 1940.

Völker, W., *Fortschritt und Vollendung bei Philo von Alexandrien (Texte und Untersuchungen zur Geschichte der altchristlichen Literatur*, Bd. 49), Leipzig, 1939.

Wehrli, F., *Zur Geschichte der allegorischen Deutung Homers im Altertum*, Basel, 1928.

Wendland, P., *Philos Schrift über die Vorsehung*, Berlin, 1892.

Wenschkewitz, H., *Die Spiritualisierung der Kultusbegriffe, Tempel, Priester und Opfer im Neuen Testament*, Leipzig, 1932.

Westcott, B., The Epistle to the Hebrews, London, 1892.

Whitaker, G. H., "ἀλήθεια in the New Testament and in Polybius," *The Expositor*, 1920.

Willms, H., ειχων: *eine begriffsgeschichtliche Untersuchung zum Platonismus, Teil I: Philo von Alexandreia*, Munster, 1935.

Wilcken, U., Mittels, L., *Grundzüge und Chrestomathie der Papyruskunde*, Leipzig-Berlin, 1912.

Windisch, H., *Der Hebräerbrief*,[2] Tübingen, 1931.

Wolff, H., "The Hermeneutics of the Old Testament," *Interpretation*, 1961.

Wolfson, H., Philo, *Foundations of Religious Philosophy in Judaism, Christianity, and Islam* I–II, Cambridge, Mass., 1947.

– *The Philosophy of the Church Fathers* I, Cambridge, Mass., 1956.

Wrede, W., *Das literarische Rätsel des Hebräerbriefes*, Göttingen, 1906.

Wuttke, G., *Melchisedech der Priesterkönig von Salem*, Giessen, 1927.

Yadin, Y., "The Dead Sea Scrolls and the Epistle to the Hebrews," *Scripta Hierosolymitana* 4, Jerusalem, 1957.

Zeller, E., *Die Philosophie der Griechen* I, Leipzig, 1903.

Indices

I: Old Testament

Genesis

1	134
2.2	66; 131; 132
2.7	68
2.8	23
2.9	25
2.19	28; 30
3.1	125
3.15	32
3.16	33
3.24	41
4.8	139
4.10	134
4.15 ff.	24
6.2 ff.	81
6.4	81
9.25	24
11.5	22; 24
11.6	24
12.5–7	72
14.17–20	123; 125; 126
15.5	125; 131
15.12	37
15.6	125; 133
15.15	34
16.2	125
18	77
20.3	68
22	96
22.2	76
22.9	125
22.16	70; 71; 125
23.40	135
27.42	32
28.7	135
28.17	29; 117

29.10	87
44.16–18	125

Exodus

1.22	116
2.11 f	136
4.1 ff.	125
12.7	116
12.23	16
14.19	16; 116
15.1	29
15.3	16
15.22	25
18.25	115
19.10	129
19.19	129
20.19	129
21.15 f.	127
22.26	24
24.6	63
24.8	111
25	58
25.40	76; 107
25.7	56
25.40	76; 107
25.7	56
25.40	105; 106; 110
26.1–14	57
26.30	30
28	59
28.35	63
28.30	121
29.4	103
29.21	103
29.22	113
29.26	113
29.27	113
29.29	113
29.31	113

29.34	113
30.6	109
32.32	118
33.14	16
33.35	113
34.28	75

Leviticus

2.1f.	53
2.14	53
3.17	49
4.2	122
4.3	62
4.5	113
5.15	122
7.6	74
8.6	103
8.22ff.	113
8.28	113
8.29	113
8.30	103
8.31	113
8.33	113
8.37	113
10.8–10	28
10.17f.	74
11.3f.	50
11.9ff.	50
11.21	50
11.22	18
11.42	50
15.18	50
16	101; 112
16.2ff.	111
16.3	111
16.6ff.	70
16.11–13	69
16.11–14	63
16.14	69; 111
16.15	69; 70; 73
16.16	73
16.17	61
16.27	73; 112
16.32	113
16.34	63
17.11	68
19.5f.	74
21.10	113
22.28	128

Numbers

3.3	113
11.1	16
12.7	117; 118
12.8	16
15.22ff.	122
15.27–31	129
19.11ff.	50
19.9ff.	101
20.17–20	108
21.6	125
23.19	23; 26; 27
25.8	68

Deuteronomy

1.31	26
4.21	118
7.9	115
8.5	27
8.15f.	126
9.17–20	118
9.9ff.	116
11.22	16
14.6f.	50
14.9f.	50
17.6	128
18.15	116
22.6	24
24.1	125
24.14	92
25.4	24
25.11f.	48
25.13	114
27.5–11	128
32.35	76
32.43	82–84
33.10	16

Joshua

1.5	66

I Samuel

15.22	52

II Samuel

2.14	81
7.14	84

148

I Kings

6 57
22.19 81
22.27 75

I Chronicles

25.8 78
29.15 135

II Chronicles

3–4 57

Job

1.6 81
2.1 81
27.6 102

Psalms

1.13 82
2.7 .... 76; 81; 84; 85; 121
4.7 76
8 .... 81; 85; 118
8.4–6 85
8.5–7 .... 80; 85; 118; 121
8.7 85
16.8–11 80
22 .... 76; 80; 86
22.22f. 86
23 76
22.23 .... 83; 86
29.1 81
32.1 126
39.13 135
40 .... 83; 84
40.6–8 .... 79; 83
40.7–9 .... 76; 92; 99
45.6f. 84
45.7 83
46.4 24
89.51 .... 81; 118
93.2 105
95 .... 76; 130
95.7–11 97
95.11 .... 130; 131
102.26–28 83
104.4 .... 75; 81
110 .... 78; 83; 120; 123

110.1 .... 80; 82; 83; 85; 119
110.4 ... 78; 79; 85; 98; 120; 121;
              123; 124; 125
141.2 102

Proverbs

2.16f. 15; 27

Isaiah

2.18 110
6.2 81
8.17f. 76; 83; 84; 86; 87
8.23 86
9.1 86
16.12 110
19.1 110
21.9 110
26.20 84
28.16 140
31.7 110
40.16 52
40.28 117
41.8 125
45.1 80
63.11f. 119

Jeremiah

23.20 93
31 .... 79; 132
31.31 87
31.31–34 99
31.33f. 76; 87; 100; 140

Ezekiel

43.2 27

Daniel

10.14 93

Hosea

2.16–19 116
6.6 52
12.10 116

Amos

3.8 27

149

Micah

6.6–8 52

Habakkuk

2.3f. 83; 85

Zechariah

3.4 81

II: Old Testament Apocrypha

The Wisdom of Solomon

9.2 117
9.8 108
10 132
10.17 16
11.24 117
13.4 117
13.10 110
18.15 16
18.24 .... 16; 59

III: New Testament

Matthew

3.17 85
4.2 116
4.15 86
4.19 116
5.26 92
6.30 127
7.11 127
12.11f. 127
12.38–40 90
24.26 116
24.37–39 90
27.43 86
27.46 86

Mark

1.11 85
1.13 116
3.14 116
9.7 85
12.34f. 85
12.35–37 80

14.34 86
14.62 85
15.24 86
15.29 86
16.19 85

Luke

1.19 81
1.45 113
1.79 86
3.22 85
12.59 92
13.15f. 127
14.3–5 127
17.26–32 90
23.35 86
24.27, 44 79

John

1.3 66
1.45 79
1.47 122
3.14 .... 90; 116
5.46 79
6.14 116
6.39 92
7.22ff. 127
8.46 122
11.24 92
12.48 92
13.15 96
19.24 86

Acts

2.17 92
2.25–29 80
2.34 85
2.36 116
3.22ff. 116
6.1 64
7 .... 64; 65
7.38 .... 76; 77
7.43f. 55
7.44 105
7.47ff. 110
7.48ff 55
7.55 77
13.33ff. 85
17.48 55

18.24–28	64
21.38	116
26.22 f.	79
28.23	79

Romans

1.17	86
3.2	76
4.6–8	126
5.14 ff.	93
5.15	89
7.14	100
8.34	85; 122
9.1	102
10.11	140
11.12	127
11.24	127
12.1	52
15.9	132
16.25	79

I Corinthians

4.4	102
5.7	93
8.6	66
9.8–10	24
10.2 ff.	93
10.6	89; 130
11.25	87
12.3	74
13.10	113
15.25	85
15.26	92

II Corinthians

3.7 ff.	94
3.8	127
3.9	127
3.11	127
3.12–16	79
3.16	75
5.21	116; 122

Galatians

3.8	131
3.11	86
3.19	77
3.22	81
4.22 ff.	93; 95

Ephesians

1.20	85
1.22	85
2.19–22	116
4.13 f.	78
6.17	67

Philippians

3.21	85

Colossians

1.16	66
1.17	67
2.16	74
2.17	104
2.21 ff.	74
3.1	85

I Timothy

1.6–7	74
3.15	116
4.3	74

II Timothy

3.1	92

Titus

1.13 ff.	74

Hebrews

1.1	92
1.2	66; 79; 82; 92; 93; 118
1.3	66; 67
1.4	81; 83
1.5	76; 81; 84; 85
1.6	76; 82; 84; 92; 96
1.7	76; 81
1.8	83; 84
1.10–12	118
1.13	76; 83; 85
1.14	81
2.2	77; 98
2.2–4	128
2.3 f.	92
2.5	81
2.68	85; 118
2.9	92; 118
2.10	113; 118

2.12f.	83; 86	6.13	70
2.13	84; 86	6.14	76
2.14	121	6.17	71; 79
2.17	120; 121; 122	6.18	71
3.1	65; 120	6.19	71; 108
3.2	116	6.20	100; 120; 124
3.2–5	117	7.1–14	126
3.3–4	66	7.1–28	78
3.3–7	130	7.2	124
3.12	130	7.3	120; 124; 125; 126
3.13	131	7.4	124
3.15	130	7.5	98; 124
3.16–19	130	7.6	124
4.1	131	7.8	100; 125
4.2f.	131	7.9f.	126
4.3	130; 131	7.10	79; 124
4.4	66; 131	7.11	71; 93; 98; 113; 120; 124
4.5	130	7.12	83; 98
4.6	131	7.14	77; 120
4.7	88; 130	7.14–16	124
4.8	130; 131	7.15	120; 124
4.10	131	7.16	100
4.11	97; 110	7.17	76; 79; 83; 124
4.12	67; 68; 78	7.19	98; 113
4.13	130	7.20	120; 124
4.14–15	120	7.21	76; 83; 85; 124
4.15	113; 122	7.22	94
5.1	120; 122	7.23	100
5.2	113; 121	7.23–25	123
5.3	96; 122; 123	7.24	100
5.4–6	121	7.25	122
5.5	76; 84; 85; 110; 120	7.26	122
5.6	78; 83	7.26–28	120
5.7	119	7.27	70; 100; 111; 122; 123
5.7–9	121	7.28	98; 100; 113; 124
5.8–10	113	8.1	120
5.9	92	8.1f.	107
5.10	78	8.2	114
5.11	62; 77	8.3	120; 122
5.11–14	78; 79	8.4	98; 120
5.11–6.3	112	8.5	76; 97; 105; 106; 110; 111
5.12	76; 79; 82	8.6	93; 94; 99
5.14	113	8.7	93
6.1	78; 79; 113	8.8	76; 93; 99; 132
6.4–6	74	8.9	93
6.4–8	129; 130	8.10	93; 100; 101; 103; 140
6.5	69	8.12	140
6.10	85; 121	9.1	93; 95; 106; 108; 109
6.12	71	9.2–5	109

9.3 .... 106; 108
9.4 99
9.6–12 91
9.6–10 94
9.7 .... 69; 111; 120
9.8 108
9.9 ....93; 95; 102; 114
9.10 .... 93; 98; 100
9.11–10.25 .... 93; 94
9.11 .... 110; 111; 114; 120
9.12 .... 93; 100; 111; 123
9.12–14 107
9.13 113
9.13f. 101; 128
9.14 .... 100; 114
9.15 ...... 93; 99; 100; 102; 132
9.18 .... 93; 111
9.19 98
9.20 111
9.22 .... 93; 98
9.23 .... 97; 111; 119
9.23f. 107
9.24 .... 111; 114; 122; 124
9.25 .... 120; 123
9.25f. 111
9.26 .... 93; 102; 122
9.28 .... 92; 96
10.1 .... 98; 104; 113; 114
10.2 .... 102; 103
10.3 .... 71; 102
10.5–10 83
10.5–7 99
10.5 .... 76; 84
10.7 79
10.8f. 99
10.10 100
10.11 .... 120; 123
10.12 .... 92; 96; 102
10.14 114
10.15 79
10.16 .... 100; 101; 103; 140
10.19f. 95
10.20 .... 94; 111
10.22 114
10.26 .... 122; 129
10.26–29 74
10.26–30 130
10.28 128
10.28f. 99

10.29 111
10.30 76
10.37–38 .... 76; 83; 85
10.39 83
11.1 133
11.3 .... 67; 93; 133
11.6 133
11.10 .... 71; 72
11.11 135
11.13 .... 115; 131
11.16 136
11.17 .... 76; 96
11.19 96
11.25f. 118
11.26 133
11.27 133
11.30–40 136
11.39 .... 115; 131; 133
11.40 115
12.2 114
12.3–11 74
12.16f. 130
12.16–17 74
12.22–24 115
12.24 .... 93; 134
12.25 129
13.5 .... 66; 76
13.8 100
13.9–10 73
13.10 110
13.11f. 112
13.13 74
13.20 100
13.20f. 119

James

5.10 96
2.21–24 125

I Peter

1.19 122
1.20 92
2.5 .... 52; 116
2.19 102
2.22 122
3.20f. 90
3.21 103
3.22 85

153

4.11	76
4.17	116

II Peter

2.6	96; 97

I John

2.1	122

Jude

7	97

Revelation

1.6	116
5.12	85
7.11	81
8.2	81
8.3f.	109
14.13	132
15.1	92
15.3f.	116
16	90
21.9	92